SMALL-CHURCH CHECKUP

ASSESSING YOUR CHURCH'S HEALTH AND CREATING A TREATMENT PLAN

By Kay Kotan and Phil Schroeder

Foreword by Dr. Lovett Weems

DISCIPLESHIP
RESOURCES

ISBNs
978-0-88177-891-5 (print)
978-0-88177-892-2 (mobi)
978-0-88177-893-9 (ePub)

Printed in the United States of America.

DR891

TABLE OF CONTENTS

PREFACE

Path 1's Wesleyan Church Planting Resources

In the summer of 2013, staff of Path 1 (New Church Starts at Discipleship Ministries of The United Methodist Church), along with a selected group of associates from around the United States, embarked on an extensive road trip. We visited more than 320 of the new churches that had been planted in the previous five years. Through hundreds of conversations with church planters and judicatory leaders of congregational development, we learned about the hopes and heartaches of starting new places for new people and revitalizing existing churches among the people called Methodist in the United States. We learned of innovative "out-of-the-box" church plants as well as traditional strategies that are reaching new people and making disciples of Jesus Christ for the transformation of the world. We celebrate the many ways annual conferences and districts of the church are finding to form new communities of faith. We also learned that there was a lack of written resources available that guided new church planting in a Wesleyan theological perspective. Thus, we set out to create Wesleyan Church Planting Resources. Our hope is that these resources will not only help those who plant new churches but will also help those who work to revitalize existing churches.

Small-Church Checkup is the sixth book to be published as part of this initiative. Kay Kotan, Director of Congregational Development for the Susquehanna Annual Conference of The United Methodist Church, and Phil Schroeder, Director of Congregational Development for the North Georgia Annual Conference, have put together a practical guide for small churches that brings hope and direction for the future of these communities of faith. We encourage a team from your church to work through this checkup together. Talk about the state of health of the church. Complete the assessment included in the appendix. Work on a plan of action for your future. This resource provides the tools that will help you put together a plan. I am convinced that you will be filled with a sense of hope and purpose by working through the steps outlined in this book.

We are grateful to Kay and Phil for sharing from their experience and expertise as they provide all the elements for a proper diagnosis of your church and a sensible plan to attain a greater measure of health going forward. I am grateful to them for their contribution to our series of books. You will be, too.

Douglas Ruffle
General Editor of Wesleyan Church Planting Resources

Other Titles in Path 1's
Wesleyan Church Planting Resources Series

A Missionary Mindset: What Church Leaders Need to Know to Reach Their Community—Lessons from E. Stanley Jones by Douglas Ruffle (Discipleship Resources, 2016).

Failing Boldly: How Falling Down in Ministry Can Be the Start of Rising Up by Christian Coon (Discipleship Resources, 2017).

Flipping Church: How Successful Church Planters Are Turning Conventional Wisdom Upside-Down, edited by Michael Baughman (Discipleship Resources, 2016).

Viral Multiplication in Hispanic Churches: How to Plant and Multiply Disciple-Making Hispanic Churches in Twenty-first Century America by Iosmar Álvarez (Discipleship Resources, 2016).

Vital Merger: A New Church Start Approach that Joins Church Families Together by Dirk Elliott (Foreword by Douglas T. Anderson), Fun & Done Press, 2013.

FOREWORD

Small churches are not new. They have abounded from the beginning of Christianity. Small churches constituted the overwhelming majority of congregations in U.S. Protestant denominations that spread across the country as the nation moved westward. Churches were established close together in a country that was seventy-five percent rural with limited travel ranges in the early twentieth century. Most of these churches continue to serve their communities, even as the population is almost eighty percent non-rural today. It hardly needs to be said that smaller churches face many challenges.

Small churches are living organisms that experience life cycles, including birth and death, growth and decline, vitality and stagnation. Therefore, churches need the same kind of nurture and care that other living things require. You will find that the categories of diagnosis and treatment options used in this book fit remarkably well for churches. All of us have known people who ignored a proper diagnosis and treatment of their physical health until it was too late. There is no reason for this to happen to churches, especially after engaging with this book.

A new factor among today's smaller churches is the rise of the very small churches, those with fifty or fewer in worship attendance. This size church is becoming more numerous each year. Despite the fact that it is from this group that almost all church closures come, there has still been an increase of almost 2,400 such United Methodist churches in the past ten years. And these constitute a majority of the denomination's congregations in the United States. Fewer of the very small churches are showing attendance increases each year. For a long time, about one-third of these churches would show attendance gains in any given year. That percentage now has fallen well below thirty percent. Every year now, there is a decline in the likelihood that a church that begins the year with fifty or fewer worshipers the past year will end the year averaging fifty-one or more in worship.

A major challenge for most small churches is to recapture the once-common multigenerational character of small churches. Churches can survive with vitality generation after generation if they can maintain a multigenerational constituency. The dilemma is seen in the high death rates within smaller churches, often twice that of the general population. The aging of membership and changes in the makeup of communities often mean that the primary source of younger members in the past—their own families—is not a source today. In all likelihood, new children and youth will not come primarily from those related to, or perhaps even known by, current members. It is from a renewed engagement with the community, especially any new neighbors, that some small churches are finding new life and hope.

I grew up in a rural Mississippi church that was part of a three-point circuit. I spent the early years of my ministry in similar circuits or in open country and small-town churches. As a seminary president and professor, I have worked with student pastors and denominational leaders who serve a preponderance of small-membership churches. Over the years, I have learned lessons about leadership and small-membership churches that I see taken very seriously in this fine book.

History is important for the small-membership church, where yesterday is usually better than they think tomorrow will be. The future needs somehow to be connected to the past. Likewise, each of these churches operates within a distinctive culture. It is not enough for solutions to be "right," but they must feel "right for us." And change is hard for small churches because change has not always been good for them and their communities. New visions and new frontiers face skepticism, often for good reason. They identify more easily with endurance and maintenance.

Innovative church leaders can take the lessons of this new volume to use in creative ways for helping congregations consider their futures. Grounded in Scripture and set in spiritual discernment, the insights and options offered here can help churches of any size see that God still has a next faithful step for them. Their task is not to become like any other church, but they must be faithful to seek and follow the next chapter that God has for their particular congregation. The current state of things—whether in the largest or smallest churches—is never synonymous with God's ultimate will. We cannot become what God wants us to be by remaining what we are.

Lovett H. Weems, Jr.
Wesley Seminary Distinguished Professor
of Church Leadership and Founding Director/Senior
Consultant, Wesley G. Douglass Lewis Center for Church
Leadership, Wesley Theological Seminary, Washington, DC

ACKNOWLEDGMENT AND DEDICATIONS

Let us take a moment here to acknowledge you. There are so many small churches that have not been brave enough to begin the process of self-examination and reflection. Few have sought out resources to explore their treatment options, given their present conditions. Please take a moment to celebrate the fact that you are reading this book. Maybe you are one who has also worked through all the chapters. Maybe you have even determined your diagnosis. Maybe you have gone so far as to choose a treatment plan. Wherever you are in the process, take a moment to celebrate. This is hard work! We want to acknowledge your persistence and bravery to have come this far. Thank you for having faith in the journey. If you have not quite made the entire trek, fear not. Continue on, faithful servant!

Dedications

For the people of Lowell UMC who were a stable small church with a ministry of training pastors and for Stark UMC and Grayson UMC who lived out a vision as not-yet-big churches to grow by meeting and welcoming their neighbors. —Phil Schroeder

With gratitude to the two Missouri small churches of Cameron UMC and Savannah UMC where my faith was sprouted. —Kay Kotan

INTRODUCTION

You probably know the projections already, but let's lay them on the table: According to an article by Charita Goshay on CantonRep.com (www.cantonrep.com/article/20150530/LIFESTYLE/150529155), in 2015, "an estimated 80 percent of churches are flat or declining; 5,600 close every year."

This is not only a sobering and startling fact, but a reality that mainline Christians are faced with on almost a daily basis. This book is not about living in the fear that our churches are closing or our denominations are coming to an end. This book is meant to be a resource that offers hope, alternatives, and the possibility of a new beginning.

As Christians, we echo the beliefs stated in the Apostles' Creed: "We believe in the Holy Spirit, the holy catholic church, the communion of saints, the forgiveness of sins, the resurrection of the body, and the life everlasting." Yes, we are believers of the Resurrection and resurrection. Yet many times, we give up on our churches. We ask you to reconsider! If you find yourself in a declining church, we ask you to consider a heart checkup. In our minds, we sometimes believe there is little or no hope, that there is no way to reach new people. If we **believe** in our hearts that there is another possibility, we are convinced we can be faithful in choosing intentional pathways forward that honor God, honor the church founders, and honor generations to come. For we, the people, are God's "Plan A" for the church's fruitfulness and vitality.

We can choose our story. We do not have to allow our story to unfold without our intervention, intentionality, faithfulness, and prayer. We **can** choose. We do not have to allow the inevitable to just happen to us and our churches. We can choose with intention the future of a church. This book is about providing options and allowing you to **choose** your future with guidance from the Holy Spirit. We believe the options (for the most part) have not been offered to most churches facing tough decisions. Therefore, many churches are not aware of other choices beyond just closing the doors after the money is gone or the last person has turned out the lights.

For the purposes of this book, when we refer to small churches, we are typically speaking of churches that have fewer than one hundred people in worship attendance. A small church might also be defined as one that is no longer able to support full-time clergy. Of course, not all small churches are the same.

Below are three different types of small churches that were identified by Douglas Walrath, Lowry Professor Emeritus of Practical Theology at the former Bangor Theological Seminary. In his book, *Making It Work: Effective Administration in the Small Church* (Judson Press, 1994), Walrath names these categories as:

1. Not Yet Big Churches (NYBC)
2. Stable Small Churches (SSC)
3. Smaller Churches (SC)

Allow us to offer our own definitions of these three distinctly different types of small churches:

Not Yet Big Churches are churches on an upward trend. They are places of hospitality. Their communities may be growing. With diligence, energy, and innovation, these churches have a real chance at growth and increased vitality.

Stable Small Churches show who they are over and over with deliberation. They are most often known for having a niche ministry and are a vital part of their community.

Smaller Churches are those that are steadily growing smaller in number. If you track their membership, they might appear to be stable, but check their fruit. Is worship attendance declining? Look back five years, ten years. How many professions of faith have they had this year? How many professions of faith did they have in the last five years? These are churches that might be on hospice care. Many times, smaller churches have lost their connection with the community. We often find smaller churches with people who are commuting back to a church where they used to live, with the church being the only reason they visit the community.

According to Daniel P. Smith and Mary K. Sellon's book, *Pathway to Renewal* (Rowman & Littlefield, 2008), smaller churches or declining congregations focus on:

- growing the church rather than witnessing to the faith
- running the church rather than forming disciples
- being people-led rather than Spirit-led
- participating in mission projects rather than having a mission
- fixing rather than creating
- ritual rather than effectiveness
- fundraising rather than generosity
- check writers rather than sharers of the good news and good deeds
- methods rather than beliefs.

Other indicators of a declining congregation include:

- deferred building maintenance
- deferred spiritual growth and/or renewal
- reduced (or no) apportionment payments (connectional giving to a larger purpose)
- continuous budget cuts
- reduction in paid staff
- reduction in clergy support

- little or no ministry budget
- making purchases on a high-interest credit card
- overly complicated and cumbersome policies
- few new groups where new people find a home
- little hands-on outreach.

During the General Conference of The United Methodist Church on May 17, 2016, Bishop Bruce Ough shared the following personal story:

"On Christmas Eve, 1973, my family and I returned home from Christmas Eve worship to find my 20-year-old brother, who had remained home with a cold, having a heart attack. He was stabilized at our local hospital. A few days later he was flown by air ambulance to the Mayo Clinic in Rochester, Minnesota. There the doctors performed open heart surgery. When they opened his heart, they discovered it was severely diseased, probably from an undiagnosed case of rheumatic fever. There was nothing the doctors could do, so they sewed up his chest. Two days later he had another heart attack. He had difficulty breathing and was placed on a ventilator. Next, his kidneys failed and he was placed on a dialysis machine. My brother, Greg, was dying. The day of decision arrived. My parents, overcome with grief and misplaced guilt, were immobilized. So at the age of 23, it fell to me to make the decision to turn off the machines keeping my brother alive. My brother died of a diseased heart, but my heart was broken. I know what it is to have a broken heart. What it feels like to have a broken heart. Many of you know what it is to have a broken heart" (www.minnesotaumc.org/newsdetail/bishop-ough-call-us-back-to-be-your-flock-together-4800556).

Many churches have broken hearts. They know how broken hearts feel. They yearn for the heydays when their churches were overflowing with people—especially children. They desire nothing more than to be vibrant congregations once again. Yet many of our churches are not willing or able to see the truth of their current reality. Often, smaller churches are stuck trying to relive the past rather than reinventing themselves for the present or future. They become chapels as they turn inward, are served by a chaplain, and are known for rituals like weddings and funerals. Chapels sometimes die because of low respiration; they have run on recycled air for years or decades, rather than the fresh air required for abundant life. Imagine breathing the same air over and over again. It becomes stale and unhealthy, leading to disease or maybe even death.

> Is your church on life support? Is it time for someone to assess the situation and choose death with certain hope of resurrection? Are you prolonging life or prolonging death?

These are difficult questions, and often we really don't want to know the answers. Yet if we are faithful people who believe in resurrection, isn't it time to ask these hard questions? Isn't it time to assess the health and vitality of your church? Isn't it time to explore your treatment options? Churches don't have to close, but for many, a lack of decision results in a slow, painful death. Churches have choices—many choices. Churches can *even* intentionally choose to close. Our hope is that this book gives you options. And in knowing your options, you can **intentionally choose** your future. There is so much power and confidence in intentional choice. You didn't just let something happen; you chose with great and faithful intent. We believe the necessity, honor, and responsibility to choose is an important story for your church, planning for your future, trusting God for new life.

Sometimes our churches simply need to start telling a different story. It may be a story of hope and vitality rather than a story of mourning the fruitful days of the past. It may need to be one of support and encouragement rather than bashing current leadership. There are some stories that need to stop being told! Sometimes it is because they are not true. Sometimes it is because the stories keep us wallowing in our grief rather than considering the future. Maybe your congregation simply needs a tongue depressor! The way your congregation talks about your church might be killing you in the community. Perception is everything, friends! Who wants to be part of a congregation that gets only bad press or seems always to have something negative going on? **How we talk about our church matters!**

Whose church is it anyway? It is great for people to love their church and want the best for it, but sometimes in our great love, we forget to whom the church belongs. It is God's church. We're the current occupants placed here to do God's work. Sometimes in viewing it as "our church," we lose sight of our responsibility to the church. We see the church as the building rather than the people. When church becomes more about the facility than the people, we lose the fight for "saving people." We must remember we are called to be stewards of both the facility and the people of our parish. Our stewardship gives us responsibility for the church **and** the community. When a church closes, too often people lament losing the building rather than mourning the loss of ministries and connections that diminish the body of Christ.

What happens in one's body when there is a heart blockage? There is normally some type of symptom: shortness of breath, weakness, lack of energy, numbness, back pain, and so on. Depending on the medical issue behind the blockage, there are a variety of treatment plans: balloon procedure, stent placement, open-heart or bypass surgery. Left untreated, someone could lose his or her life due to the blockage. At other times, the body may compensate and develop new pathways through which the blood can flow.

Does your church have a blockage?

> If so, what is the underlying cause?
> What are possible treatment options?
> Is there a possibility to create a whole new pathway to vital ministry?
> Are all the chapters of your church already written?

℞ **Daily Health Initiative 1:** Write your favorite story about your church. Share it with at least one person each day this week.

We invite you to a day of new beginnings.

(Sing or read aloud the first verse of "This Is a Day of New Beginnings," *United Methodist Hymnal*, 383.)

A WORD OF WARNING!

Do not try this alone!

Pastors, do not go about this alone.
Laity, do not go about this alone.

The journey you are about to undertake is a journey that requires collaboration, prayer, patience, and the willingness to be uncomfortable. Before embarking, gather the pastor and a team of laity who are willing to take this journey without really knowing the journey's destination. This is a journey of discernment of God's future vision for your church. This journey will take some courage and tenacity to endure. This journey will take brave, mature, committed, faithful souls to seek God's preferred future for your church. This is not a journey for one. This is not a journey for two or three. This is a journey for a team. Gather your journey team. Choose wisely.

Chapter One
THE PHYSICAL

There was a man of the Pharisee sect, Nicodemus, a prominent leader among the Jews. Late one night he visited Jesus and said, "Rabbi, we all know you're a teacher straight from God. No one could do all the God-pointing, God-revealing acts you do if God weren't in on it."

—John 3: 1-2, MSG

The first step in recovery is accepting the truth. What is the truth about our church's current condition? What is true, but has not been said out loud? What have we denied? Where have we not been faithful? Where have we been unwilling to move outside our comfort zones to reach new people? Where are we stuck?

It is recommended that we all have annual physicals with our doctors for preventive measures and early diagnosis. Yet many people don't act on this recommendation, even when physicals are covered in full by most health insurance plans. You may have heard your grandmother say, "An ounce of prevention is worth a pound of cure."

When we go for our annual physicals, we expect certain procedures. First, we get the clipboard where we offer personal information, health history, current medications, and current presenting issues. Next, the nurse calls us back and starts the routine, taking temperature, blood pressure, pulse, respiration rate, height, and weight. Then the nurse asks if there are any issues that need to be addressed—aches, pains, and worries. All of this information is placed on the chart for future reference.

When the doctor FINALLY enters the room, the patient waits for a turn to talk, as the doctor reviews the chart. At this point, the doctor may order tests–laboratory, x-rays, MRI. The doctor may recommend a new regimen to follow right away or after testing and diagnosis is complete. The patient may walk away from the appointment without answers or with more questions. He or she might walk away with a referral to a specialist of some sort.

When was the last time your church had a physical—a checkup to evaluate its health? We believe we fully understand our current health, but we may have a distorted perception of our true wellbeing.

What Are Your Church's Symptoms? (Check all that apply)

Loss of appetite for new people	Decreased worship attendance	No professions of faith
No/few children	No new Sunday school classes	No new small groups
Lack of volunteers	High staff turnover	Budget worries/ deficits
Deferred building maintenance	Church doesn't reflect mission field demographics	Negative/no community perception
Lack of guests	Traditionalism trumps innovation	Lack of missional focus

When it comes to examining the health of your church, gathering vital signs is critical.

- You need to know the temperature of your church—its spiritual maturity.
- You need to know the pulse of your church—the average worship attendance and how many people visit the church and how often.
- What is the respiration rate—the number of professions of faith?
- What is your church's blood pressure? How are you caring for those inside the church and how are you engaging with the community or mission field outside the church?

Average worship attendance and professions of faith are easy to measure, but spiritual maturity and missional engagement are more difficult. However, you know it when you see it in the behavior and narratives.

Here is a method to measure spiritual maturity: Listen to your church. What stories are told over and over again? Are you hearing stories of winners and losers or stories of grace and kingdom impact? Do you talk *to* people or *about* them? Do you emerge from meetings unified despite your differences of opinion, or do you spin your displeasure about decisions back through the grapevine?

Call to Action:
Complete the "Your Church Health History" assessment on page 123 in the Appendix.

Here are some ways to measure missional impact: When decisions (i.e., worship style, worship times, new ministries, youth activities, mission trips) are made in your church, whose interests are considered? Make a list:

1.
2.
3.
4.
5.

How many listed are the interests of people outside the church? Are the interests of those outside the church considered at all? Which generation's concerns predominate? We know that most people make a profession of faith before they are twenty-one years old. Are we considering how our decisions influence the next generation of Christians, or do we tend to please those who have already found faith?

Think about the story you wrote down as your first health initiative? Did it have to do with things happening inside the church or outside the church?

Phil Schroeder talks about his experience working with a church that was struggling with its early worship service:

> I asked them to talk about the decision-making process for starting the service. They admitted to choosing the time that was easiest for them to avoid making any shifts in their current worship times. I asked how they decided who preached the service. This admission was more difficult, but they finally stated, "We had a few disgruntled associates who did not get to preach enough, so we let them rotate through this service."
>
> The service was not designed for the people in the community, but for the convenience of the church. No

wonder it was struggling to grow! After our time together, the church designated one associate as the pastor of that service and chose a time that was most convenient for the young families in the community. That worship service now continues to grow and thrive.

Consider whom you serve. According to church consultant Ken Callahan, most churches serve more people than they think. What are the various ways your church interacts with people outside the walls of the church? Consider those served in mission, constituents, members, people in the community, and friends of the congregation who live elsewhere. Here are some examples from Ken Callahan to help you think through each of these categories:

People Served in Mission

- Direct help for hopes and hurts in the grace of God and on behalf of the congregation
- A direct relationship
- Hospital visits
- Community mission projects
- Weddings
- Funerals
- Shepherding emergencies

Constituents

- Nonmembers who participate in one or more church activities

- Children who are not yet members
- Nonmembers who think of themselves as members

Members

- Resident members who are at least marginally active in the life of the church

People in the Community

- People who think well of your church and its mission
- People who offer support when it serves some distinct mission in the community
- People who use the building for a non-church related activity (i.e., scouts, exercise, recovery groups, etc.)

Friends of the Congregation

- Live elsewhere
- Still view the congregation as home
- Were blessed by this congregation while they lived here.

Considering the categories above, complete the chart for your church activities below. Think about how many people are being served through that activity, the number of people who participate in providing the activity, and the number of people from the community who are affected by the activity. This chart will serve as a snapshot of the "people impact" of the activities where your church chooses to invest its time and resources.

Activity Name	# of People Serving	# of People Participating	# of People from Community Impacted

There are many people who may offer a diagnosis for your church. One of my favorites is the "church shut-in." She is "shut-in" only from church. You may see her at the grocery store, the local restaurant, or the beauty parlor. But she complains you don't come to see her because she is a shut-in. Another person who might offer an unsolicited diagnosis is the former pastor or the longtime church secretary.

While these diagnoses can be helpful, more often they are inwardly directed, narrowly defined, and counterproductive. Churches must be careful about which voices they allow to be the sources of their diagnoses. Sometimes internal and uninformed diagnoses are self-fulfilling or even self-serving. Anyone can provide a diagnosis, so seek wise counsel from qualified experts rather than from amateurs. Invite unchurched people that you trust from the community to mystery worship at your church to give their impressions of the welcome. Diagnosis is only half the equation. Diagnosis without a treatment plan is futile.

There are times we are so overwhelmed with symptoms and pain that we become paralyzed. At this point, people are telling you what's wrong, but they have no idea how to fix it. Even medical professionals do not always agree on a common diagnosis and/or treatment. We might feel the need to call in a patient advocate to help us navigate the diagnosis and treatment. An advocate helps us navigate the various diagnoses, test results, treatments, competing medications, and conflicting opinions to find a way forward. The passage from John 14 offers another advocate—the Spirit of Truth.

> If you love me, show it by doing what I've told you. I will talk to the Father, and he'll provide you another Friend so that you will always have someone with you. This Friend is the Spirit of Truth. The godless world can't take him in because it doesn't have eyes to see him, doesn't know what to look for. But you know him already because he has been staying with you, and will even be *in* you! (John 14:16-17, MSG)

This book can be your advocate, but please don't overlook the possibility of seeking an outside consultant who has a proven track record of helping churches.

In the history of the church, we have often spoken of the sacrament of confession, but the name of the sacrament is actually reconciliation. Confession is the diagnosis, and penitence is the treatment. God's grace is ultimately the cure.

Here is a precaution as you enter into the journey: Don't diagnose without proper history and tests and at least one second opinion. Don't start a treatment plan until you have a proper, well-informed diagnosis. Do your work in logical order for the best results.

At the beginning of the Communion liturgy, there is always an act of confession. It doesn't begin with forgiveness, but confession and an act of pardon. Neither should be used without the other.

The order is critical. Just as the order of the Communion liturgy is important, the order for this journey is important as well. At the beginning of church renewal, we have to confess where we have failed to be an obedient church.

Confession (from "Service of Word and Table I," *The United Methodist Book of Worship*)

Merciful God,
we confess that we have not loved you with our whole
    heart.
We have failed to be an obedient church.
We have not done your will,
    we have broken your law,
    we have rebelled against your love,
    we have not loved our neighbors,
    and we have not heard the cry of the needy.
Forgive us, we pray.
Free us for joyful obedience,
    through Jesus Christ our Lord. Amen.[1]

Then we pray in silence.

What does your church need to confess today? This is where you begin to understand your diagnosis. Are you loving your neighbor? Do you hear the cry of the needy? Are you an obedient

---

1. From "Service of Word and Table I," *The United Methodist Book of Worship*, page 35, Copyright © 1992 The United Methodist Publishing House. Used with permission.

church? Have you loved God with your whole heart? Where have you fallen short?

$\text{R}_{\!x}$ **Daily Health Initiative 2:** What does your church need to confess? Share this with another person from your church for the next week.

Look at the chart below. Circle the words used most frequently in conversations in your church.

Is	What we are doing	What God is calling us to do	Future	Looking forward
Was	What we might do	What God calls us to do	Present	Looking backward
Is to come	What we did	What God is calling us to do	Past	Looking at today

We are believers in a Christ that was, is, and is to come (paraphrase of Rev. 1:8). As you think about your church, what do the conversations there center around? If you place a stethoscope over your church's heart and listen closely, what you do hear? What do you hear in board meetings? In announcements? Are you talking about what you have done, what you are doing, or what you will be doing next?

What is God's hope for your church's future? Perhaps that's the wrong question. **What is God's hope for God's church's future?** Are most of the words circled in the box above rooted in your history, your present, or your future? What words might be helpful to introduce into new conversations?

If you are struggling with these questions, consider this: Søren Kierkegaard, a Danish theologian, also struggled with these same questions in the mid-1800s. He asked who the audience is for worship. Most people would respond that we, the congregation, are the audience. The way we talk about worship and evaluate the quality of it at lunch afterward surely confirms that we believe we are the audience for worship. Kierkegaard challenged the people of his day to consider that God is the audience for worship. We come to offer our sacrifice of praise. We offer worship to God. We are the actors of worship, prompted by the pastors and musicians. If God is the audience, God needs to be pleased by the worship we offer. When we walk out after church on Sunday, we need to ask if God was pleased with what we offered in worship, not if we were pleased with worship.

"The Bible is very easy to understand. But we Christians are a bunch of scheming swindlers. We pretend to be unable to understand it because we know very well that the minute we understand, we are obliged to act accordingly."
—*Provocations: Spiritual Writings of Kierkegaard*
www.relevant magazine.com

A Story from Phil Schroeder

My 87-year-old mother gives an offering to her church every week. Did you know there are people like that? She gives her tithe on the first Sunday and continues to give over and above that for the rest of the month. When I asked her why she did this (tithing on the first Sunday and giving away my inheritance on the others), she replied, "I wouldn't feel like I had worshiped if I didn't give." Each Sunday she prays that God will be pleased with what she offered that day, both her gift and her praise.

To move from a smaller church to a stable, small church, to a not-yet-big church, or to a totally new way of being the church (like Fresh Expressions, http://freshexpressionsus.org), we must be willing to make some basic shifts. We must ask, **"Will God be pleased with our decisions even when we are not?"** This is a step toward spiritual growth and maturity. How many times have we prayed, "Let the words of my mouth and the meditations of my heart be pleasing to you, Lord, my rock, and my redeemer?" (Psalm 19:14, CEB) or echoed Luke 22:42, "not my will, but thine, be done."

Now that you have had a thorough physical examination and have reached the first impressions, it is time to move into the next phase of the exam—the consultation.

Chapter Two

THE CONSULTATION

"Moses said to his father-in-law, "Because the people come to me with questions about God. When something comes up, they come to me. I judge between a man and his neighbor and teach them God's laws and instructions."

Moses' father-in-law said, "This is no way to go about it. You'll burn out, and the people right along with you. This is way too much for you—you can't do this alone. Now listen to me. Let me tell you how to do this so that God will be in this with you. Be there for the people before God, but let the matters of concern be presented to God. Your job is to teach them the rules and instructions, to show them how to live, what to do. And then you need to keep a sharp eye out for competent men—men who fear God, men of integrity, men who are incorruptible—and appoint them as leaders over groups organized by the thousand, by the hundred, by fifty, and by ten. They'll be responsible for the everyday work of judging among the people. They'll bring the hard cases to you, but in the routine cases they'll be the judges. They will *share your load and that will make it easier for you. If you handle the work this way, you'll have the strength to carry out whatever God commands you, and the people in their settings will flourish also."*

—Exodus 18:15-23, MSG

During an examination, your doctor reviews your health history, asks questions about your current symptoms, and inquires about how you are feeling–all subjective measures of the consultation. During this time, information is compared against prevailing symptoms, which might be compared to your overall feeling of health. Consulting is the act of looking for information. For a doctor, the consultation is a search for information through the lens of education and experience.

Health History

Look at your church's health history (see the Appendix, page 119). Do any of the answers surprise you? If so, which ones and why? Where do you need more information or understanding? Who needs to hear about your discoveries and why?

Current Symptoms

To analyze current symptoms in the church, George Bullard, author of *The Congregational Life Cycle Assessment*, asks what influences decision making in your church. Vision? Relationships? Ministries? Structure? Why are these four components important? According to Bullard's life cycle of a church, these are the four components— vision, relationships, ministries/programs, and structure—that make up the life of the church. Understanding these components and measuring the presence of each is vital in evaluating where your church is in the life cycle. When vision drives your church, your church is growing. When vision isn't driving your church, your church's life cycle is in decline. When new relationships drive your church, you're in a growing side of the life cycle, especially if relationships are formed not only inside the church, but also *outside* with new people. If your church's driving force is structure (budget, policies, building) or programs/ministries, you're most likely on the declining side of the life cycle.

All four of these components are important in the life of the church, but a healthy balance is important when considering your church's organization and function. When all four components are well balanced, the church is at its prime. Yet, without a new vision at its prime, the church can plateau and will eventually decline if leaders are not careful.

When most churches reach their prime, they want to hit the cruise control button. Leaders don't want to change anything because they believe they have everything figured out. But without change, they fall into unrealized decline. Without change, they lose relevance within the community. Without change, they fall into ruts. The further the decline, the more difficult it is to recover and start a new life cycle. Therefore, monitoring where a church is in its life cycle is critical! Monitoring helps leaders stay in touch with reality and allows them to make needed shifts by paying attention to any of the four components they have neglected or focused on too much.

Take some time to review the life cycle of your church. Where is your church in the cycle? What brings you to that conclusion? Where was the church in the life cycle when you became part of the congregation? Share your thoughts with others. Compare and discuss your conclusion with other church attendees and leaders.

For more information, go to www.stpaulsgb.org/filerequest /2448, or read *The Congregational Life Cycle Assessment*.

℞   **Daily Health Initiative 3**: Today, do you see God at work in the life of your congregation? Share this sighting with a different person each day this week. (Share this initiative, using Facebook, Instagram, and Twitter.)

How Are You Feeling Today?

Another way to assess your church's health is to answer the question, "How is your church 'feeling' today?" When you are in the hospital, you might be asked to assess your pain on a pain assessment tool that ranks pain on a scale of zero (no pain) to ten (a great deal of pain).

Where is your church on the pain scale? Compare your reflections with others from your congregation. Discuss why you chose that particular level.

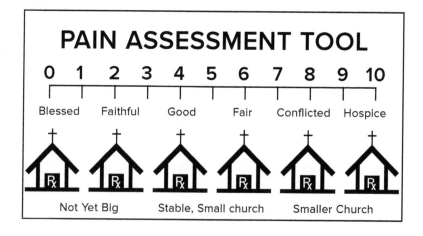

If you are to the left of center, you need to claim your ministry and do some visioning. But if you end up right of center, you are experiencing loss, **whether you are aware of it or not**. It's important to be brutally honest with one another as you talk about how you are feeling as a church. We often have pain that is not discussed. Maybe you're feeling the pain of the church and believe others are not, while others are feeling the same level of pain and are not talking about it either. This is a time to be brutally honest with one another to gain the best insights.

Loss and Grief

When people experience loss, that loss manifests itself in some form of grief. Let's review the progressive stages of grief:

1. Shock
2. Denial
3. Anger
4. Depression and detachment
5. Dialogue and bargaining
6. Acceptance
7. Return to meaningful life

Churches, like people, can experience grief. Sometimes a church recognizes it is in the grieving process; but many times, the grief is unidentified or unnamed. Understanding that organizations, like individuals, can and do grieve is important. With that recognition comes the ability to move through the stages of grief. In moving through the grieving process, churches can once again return to meaningful life.

Here are some examples of the various phases of church grief: When a church is in *shock*, it might find it unbelievable that a particular family left the church or that some type of misconduct occurred. A church in *denial* chooses not to believe or admit the current reality, such as consistent decline, or uncompelling worship. A church can be *angry* with the last pastor, the conference office, the community, or with people who have left. An angry church may feel victimized. Anger may present itself with passive aggression when what it needs is pastoral assertiveness. A church experiencing *depression and detachment* often feels defeated, resulting in a lack of energy and passion. Church members will need a quick, easy win that will help them regain their confidence that they can achieve something. The church in the *dialogue and bargaining* stage may have members who tell the pastor that the church will be fine if only the pastor will bring back the people who have left the church in the past three years (often those people left before the pastor got there). A church that is nearing the end of the grieving period has come full circle and has begun to *accept* current reality. It is only after a church has worked through the acceptance of loss (even if pain still remains) that it can begin to *return to meaningful life* and become a faithful, vital congregation.

In the midst of grief, both recognized and unrecognized, we tend to call for a change of leadership rather than dealing with the underlying symptoms, like a church that chose to paint the piano rather than tune it. One wise pastor said that instead of churches changing and growing, they change pastors. Pastors, often thinking that the grass will be greener at the next church, change churches. So neither the pastors nor the churches mature and grow. Both are stuck in an endless cycle, transferring the issue to the next person or place rather than dealing with the underlying causes, delaying acceptance or even escalating the cycle of grief.

Phil Schroeder's Story

As pastor at Grayson UMC in Grayson, Georgia, I was challenged with a growing congregation and facility limitations. In the midst of dreaming of a new building on our campus, the question was raised as to why we had not torn down the oldest building on campus. It was the original 100+-year-old chapel sitting on one acre at the corner of the property. Even though the chapel had black mold, asbestos, and was infested with squirrels, it was a beloved chapel, full of memories. Many from the congregation had been married or baptized there. People remembered just where they had sat at funerals for loved ones in this chapel. It was time for a crucial conversation. We invited an open forum for people to debate the future of this building. Many tearfully shared precious memories and pleaded for the building to remain. The last to speak were Mary and Bill Johnson. No one had been members longer. The Johnsons were in their nineties and had to hold one another up to stand before the congregation. Mary started out by sharing that she and Bill had courted in that old building. (I did not like where I thought this was headed.) Mary went on to say words that are forever etched in my memory: "We would be so sad to see this building torn down. But we wouldn't be sorry. Because it is the people of this church that we love . . . not this building."

She taught me something profound that day. Mary's comment taught me that if you live long enough and love long enough, you are going to have pain. You are going to have grief. You are going to have sorrow. To be sad, but not sorry is a pretty good way to live. My mother would agree. She has been a widow for over twenty-seven years. There is not a day that goes by that she doesn't miss my father with a twinge of sadness and the occasional tear. But she lives without any regret for the life and love they shared together.

As you move forward to make decisions about your church, there will be sadness no matter what you decide. It is our prayer that you can be sad, but not sorry. What will it take for you to deal with the sadness of change without being sorry?

We have now concluded the consultation portion of the examination—based on the information you have provided. It is now time for the next phase of the examination, where we look at labs and other test results to get a clear picture of the overall health of your church.

Chapter Three
LAB AND TEST RESULTS

Lord, you have examined me. You know me. You know when I sit down and when I stand up. Even from far away, you comprehend my plans. You study my traveling and resting. You are thoroughly familiar with all my ways. There isn't a word on my tongue, Lord, that you don't already know completely. You surround me—front and back. You put your hand on me. That kind of knowledge is too much for me; it's so high above me that I can't fathom it.

Examine me, God! Look at my heart! Put me to the test! Know my anxious thoughts! Look to see if there is any idolatrous way in me, then lead me on the eternal path!

—Psalm 139:1-6, 23-24, CEB

"Mirrors that hide nothing hurt me. But this is the hurt of purging and precious renewal—and these are the mirrors of dangerous grace."

—Walter Wangerin Jr., *Reliving the Passion*

When a patient has presenting symptoms, the doctor will often order tests to either form or confirm a diagnosis. The more complicated the symptoms, the more tests might be needed. Sometimes the tests are conducted in the doctor's office. But, most often, they're conducted outside, particularly when a specialty test is ordered or the doctor's office does not have the equipment, personnel, or expertise to run it. The doctor can't limit his or her knowledge to testing and information available only inside the office. For the patient's best interest and health, the doctor calls on tests conducted outside the office for a comprehensive picture. Testing provides another level of information gathering.

There are a variety of tests that doctors might order, including lab tests, x-rays, MRIs, EKGs, CT-scans, ultrasounds, PET scans, colonoscopies, biopsies, and a variety of others. Likewise, churches should conduct testing on a regular basis to ensure disease prevention and optimum health.

Testing is composed of objective measures. The x-ray shows if the bone is broken or not. Blood tests show if blood levels are normal or not.

Below are a few tests a church may conduct to obtain some objective measures of health. For a more complete list, please see the Appendix, page 127.

- Membership Mapping: This is a test that plots where your congregation currently resides. It provides information about where congregants live and indicates how well the people in the community are connected to the church. It also indicates how far away the majority of your people live from the church.

- Average worship attendance: What is your current average worship attendance? What are the trends in the church's worship attendance?

- Financials: Print or assemble a current balance sheet for your church. Make sure you include **all** church assets— real estate, checking accounts, money market accounts, endowments, trustee accounts, scholarship accounts, hold accounts, stocks, bonds, and so on. Compare the current balance sheet to the year-end balance sheets from five and ten years ago. Is there an increase or decrease in assets? Are the reserves slowly fading away? Print or assemble a current profit and loss statement. Compare that to the same statements from the past several years. What trending history did you discover?
- Best Sundays: Take a look at the highest worship attendance Sundays outside of Easter and Christmas. When are those Sundays? What do they seem to indicate? Are they designed for the people in your church or to connect with the community?
- Building usage: Who is in and out of the building on a weekly/monthly basis? Who uses the building? What are your relationships with them?

℞ **Daily Health Initiative 4**: Recall who handed you the baton of faith in this church. What were they willing to do to connect with you? Share your story with a new person from the church each day. Share your story with at least one person who is not connected with your church.

Daily Prayer Initiative: What prayer do you have for your church? Write it down. Pray this prayer every day for the upcoming months. Are you praying for a time machine to go backward? Are you praying to a God that makes all things new? Consider Revelation 21:5 (Look, I'm making all things new).

Chapter Four

CRUCIAL CONVERSATIONS AND FIELD TRIPS

A certain man was there who had been sick for thirty-eight years. When Jesus saw him lying there, knowing that he had already been there a long time, he asked him, "Do you want to get well?" The sick man answered him, "Sir, I don't have anyone who can put me in the water when it is stirred up. When I'm trying to get to it, someone else has gotten in ahead of me." Jesus said to him, "Get up! Pick up your mat and walk."

—John 5:5-8, CEB

Sometimes after our initial examination, the doctor sends us out to gather more information. This could include tests, getting a second opinion, or maybe even seeing a specialist. You might live in a smaller community and need to travel to a larger community to see a specialist or a more experienced doctor. Maybe you need more sophisticated testing than is available locally. We must be willing to gather all the pertinent information before we make critical decisions about our health.

Self-Advocate

Kay Kotan

One thing I have learned over the past few years is the importance of being your own advocate when it comes to your health. At one critical health juncture, my husband was seeing six different specialists. The doctors were excellent in their given fields, but concentrated only in their area of expertise. To exacerbate the dilemma, my husband was hospitalized and assigned a hospitalist (pretty much a general practitioner these days). While I am sure the hospitalist was a fine doctor, he had no history with my husband and concentrated on treating him for the presenting symptoms that brought him to the hospital. Then, there were specialists brought into the case from the hospital staff to make things even more complicated. We were given conflicting information, opinions, and treatment plans. After two days trying to navigate these difficult waters, we decided to call in the patient advocate. At the time, we did not realize we were calling in the "doctor police." We simply needed someone who would take the time to look at the whole case and help us navigate through the contradictory medications, opinions, diagnoses, and treatment plans. So, you see, there were three levels of patient advocacy going on here. First, my husband was confused by some contradictory information and needed help. Second, my husband and I started asking questions of our floor nurse, which got the ball rolling toward the patient advocate. Third, the patient advocate came in, straightened out the contradictory information, and came up with a game plan that everyone caring for my husband could agree on. All three levels were necessary to communicate and create a cohesive plan.

So, what does self-advocating look like for a church? First, you must be willing to see your current reality. Second, you need to second-guess ideas or decisions and ask more questions. Third, you need to call in the appropriate people who can help guide you. Fourth, you need to continue asking questions and listen carefully. Fifth, you must advocate until you have an acceptable solution.

Churches need to constantly evaluate and adjust their ministry plans to faithfully pursue the mission of making new disciples of Jesus Christ for the transformation of the world. A congregation cannot depend on pastors to be solely responsible for the church's fruitfulness. The pastor leads the flock—she doesn't do all the ministry herself or for you. The pastor equips the congregation to do ministry. We cannot depend on our judicatory staff (i.e., district superintendents or conference staff) to provide all the latest training, tools, and resources for all our churches. Their job is one of support and supervision. We cannot depend on conferences and general boards to make us whole. All these folks are great resources and ultimately want all churches to be fruitful congregations, but congregations cannot wait for everything to be brought to them. Churches must pursue their own resources. They must take a hard look at the effectiveness of their ministries. They must continuously retool to keep up with the changing world. Congregations must be their own advocates!

Too often, we accept what is told to us as the absolute truth. Do we check facts? Do we bury our heads in the sand and deny reality?

Do we really think that if we ignore the situation it will go away? Of course not! Many times, it becomes worse. So many times, our churches believe rumor over fact. Information is not fact-checked. Sometimes we think we know the facts, but our facts are skewed because we view the world through our "Christian glasses." We have lost touch with our community because we live and breathe inside our little Christian bubbles. How much time do you spend with unchurched people in comparison to the time you spend with churched people? We often base our beliefs about the community on our interaction with the churched rather than the unchurched. We assume things about our communities without doing the demographic work or the hands-on research. This practice is not helpful when we are trying to reach new people if we make decisions on how to reach them based on the preferences of those already with us.

Crucial Conversations

A call from a doctor's office notifying you of the need to go over test results tends to produce anxiety. We sense the news might not be positive. We worry until the time of the appointment. It's time for a crucial conversation. We've also had those crucial conversations with loved ones, times when that special person in our life proclaims, "We need to talk!" When those words are uttered, we know it's a high-stakes conversation. It could even be life-changing. These conversations take us out of our comfort zones. You may need to be with someone in a different environment or setting to have this conversation. Pulling yourself out of the norm is important for crucial conversations to be effective or maybe even just heard.

Because these conversations are critical, we tend to avoid them. Who loves conflict? However, through these important discussions, we can make great strides forward. New understandings come to pass. New possibilities are dreamed. Bridges are built. Critical situations can be avoided if we embrace the needed conversations. Avoidance does not mean the elimination of pain. Avoidance just increases the pain that comes later.

Jesus had crucial conversations with his disciples, but sometimes the disciples did not want to listen!

Are there any *crucial* conversations your church needs to have or has been avoiding? Are there any *critical* conversations you ignored that are now in need of a *crucial conversation*? Think and pray about it. What are the topics of those conversations? Who needs to be included?

When we ask questions, are we doing so with a critical eye, or through the eyes of the cross, with critique or sacrifice? Without sacrifice, there is no grace. Are you planting seeds for the future through your conversations? Do the crucial conversations end with a plan to move forward in the most faithful way possible?

Until we are transparent with where we are and what everyone is feeling, facts are checked, and level-headed conversations are had, we cannot move forward. The root of *crucial* is *crux* or *cross*. A church having a crucial conversation is at a crossroad. The word *critical* comes from the root word of *crisis*.

Time for a Field Trip

A "field trip" when seeking a conclusive medical diagnosis might mean traveling to see a specialist. The specialist might be in your town, but you might have to travel to another location. A field trip might include seeking a second opinion. Field trips seek outside

To plant is to place your plan at the foot of the cross.

expertise. You can't take your own vital signs. The field trip provides an outside measuring stick.

School children often take field trips so that they can experience the world in a different way. They might see a new town, visit a museum or learning center, or experience something they have never done before. A field trip opens up a person's world and provides new perspective, new knowledge, new understanding, and the opportunity to meet new people. You have the opportunity to see things done in a new way. Field trips take you outside your norm. A field trip interrupts the routine. Field trips are a growth opportunity, an adventure. In fact, Edwin Friedman, a therapist and leadership consultant, said that we cannot think our way out of our problems. It is only through adventure that we discover new categories in which to see our present reality.

Jesus took his disciples on field trips. In Matthew 16, he took his disciples to the district of Philippi, a place known for "other" gods. He also had crucial conversations with his disciples, "Who do people say the son of man is?" and, "Who do you say that I am." Jesus demonstrated that sometimes *where* the conversations happen matters. In John 4, Jesus was in Samaria where he sat at the well with a woman. He held up a mirror to help her see her current reality. As a result of that crucial conversation on her turf, she converted a whole community based on her experience and Jesus' question. Field trips can potentially help us think and experience life in a whole new way.

Now let's consider a field trip for your church. What possible field trips might help you discover new methods, ideas, perspectives, initiatives, and people to disrupt your current norm? Below are some possible field trips for your church to take to gain a clearer picture of your own church's current reality. It might even give you insight into a potential new future.

- Pit Stop: On the way to a church function (i.e., mission trip, United Methodist Women's or Men's district meeting), make a pit stop to use the bathroom at a church with a facility that's modern and houses a growing congregation. This is an indirect opportunity for a facility tour, allowing people to experience something they might not experience another way. It can be eye-opening. Many churched people just do not have the chance to experience other churches very often. They see church only through their own context. This field trip allows them to experience something new in a nonthreatening way. A different style of church is no longer a theory; they have seen it in the flesh. Some people just need to see to understand.

55

- Pictures: Whether it is a "pit stop" or another field trip, take pictures. Pictures allow those who participated a means of sharing their experiences and stories with others who did not make the trip.

- Experiences in Churches: Visit churches that are following the practices of fruitful congregations. Experience radical hospitality. Experience a modernized facility with great hospitality and good space and ministry for children and youth. Experience passionate worship. Experience extravagant generosity where churches have giving kiosks and are willing to talk about stewardship. Experience *risk-taking* service. Experience a church with small groups demonstrating intentional faith development. Too often, we have good people who love their churches that have never seen an alternative, so they remain stuck in their present reality.

- Experiences in the Community: Go to a local restaurant known for its hospitality. Spend a mealtime watching the interactions among the staff and customers. What keeps people coming back? Talk to the owner or operator and ask, "What do you wish churches knew about hospitality and welcome?" Visit a small-town dinner that has endured for years. Try to understand the secret of its success. Drop in on the local gym or Crossfit place that is booming and witness how it has created community.

- Next Step: Visit healthy churches that are a step or two ahead of your church on the growth curve.

- Competing church: You know the one! It's the church that people in your community talk about where "everyone" attends. Dispel myths about other "competing" churches. What do you think you know about them? Then visit the competing church. After the visit, talk about what you found. Were your assumptions founded or unfounded? Pray for that church because it is not really the competition!

- Growing: What are other churches doing to successfully reach new people? What do they do that is different from your church? What makes those churches appealing? Are they reaching the same people you are trying to reach?

- Community: Go out into your community. Conduct interviews and have conversations. Ask these questions: "What do you know about the church? What kind of impact does the church have in the community? What do you wish you knew about the church?"

- Judicatory: It might be helpful to speak to your district superintendent to gain a different perspective. What light could the district superintendent shed on the situation from a "balcony perspective" with those working down on the "dance floor" below?

- Facility pictures: Have someone from the outside shoot some pictures of your church facility (no need for a professional photographer). What have the pictures captured that might need to be addressed? Share the pictures and findings with the church. We can become desensitized to the things we see every day, overlooking the messes we make or the places where repairs are needed. When a group of trustees sees pictures taken around their own church, they often have difficulty identifying where the pictures were taken. Places where there has been a lack of care are glaringly obvious to visitors.

- Mystery Worshiper: Invite some unchurched people in your neighborhood to come worship with you and give you some honest feedback. What did they like? Dislike? What about the experience made them feel comfortable? Uncomfortable? Consider contracting with Faith Perceptions, which provides mystery worshipers to churches to evaluate a variety of different perceptions of your church from an unchurched person's perspective. Visit www.FaithPerceptions.com for more information. Or send your people out as mystery worshipers so that they can experience what it feels like to be new to a church. When they return, they may see their own settings with new eyes.

- Name it and claim it: After you've spent some time studying your mission field, claim it. What part of town is God calling you to reach? What must you do to reach these people? Is your church willing to do whatever it takes to reach them? Are you willing to change for the sake of the mission? What are the limitations to the change you can endure? Is the pain level of your current situation high enough to change what needs to be changed?

- Get personal: Sometimes you need to sit down and have a conversation with yourself. Am I part of the solution? Am I part of the problem? What needs to grow inside of me for this to happen?

- Cemetery: If the church has a cemetery, walk out and have a conversation with the departed saints—the cloud of witnesses. What would they ask of you today? What would they say about the state of the church today? Sometimes we believe we are letting our parents and grandparents down if we change. Yet it was our grandparents and great-grandparents who paved the way to do new things to reach new people. What would they ask us to do today that would make us the next pioneers? Could allowing the church to die in its current state allow for the birth of something new?

- Get real: Does your church really need to grow? If so, why? If not, why? Are the motives for either self-serving or

God-serving? Occasionally, churches will say they need to grow so they can have more people to help pay for things!

Urgent or Important

In today's fast-paced culture, we seem to move at an ever-increasing pace. We want it done yesterday. We are a society of instant gratification. We expect things instantaneously. Yet it is that very pace that trips us up. We get going so fast that we fall over our own feet. We become our own obstacle. We get swept up in the race and forget the purpose for the race or even the intended destination.

How are we spending time as a church? As leaders? Are we tending to the daily fires of the church—phone calls, drop-ins, nursing home calls, emails, voicemails—the seemingly urgent ministry? We are expected to handle the situation "right now." When we constantly get sucked into the urgent, we lose focus on the important. When we lose focus on the important, we make decisions that do not use our time, talents, gifts, and resources wisely. We begin to be about the busy-ness or tasks and lose sight of our purpose. Before long, we are really busy doing things, but we are not doing anything to fulfill the Great Commission. We can turn our focus to the important, using our time to live out the purpose of the church, making disciples of Jesus Christ for the transformation of the world.

What is the return on God's investment? God created humans to love and worship God. As humans, we are called to share Christ with others. Are we using our time, talents, gifts, and resources to honor God with an appropriate return on God's investment? Are we using the blessings of our church facility to reach new people? Are we using the gifts God has brought to us through the people of the congregation to bless others? Are we providing God with a return on investment that pleases God?

A Sense of Urgency

If your church is in decline or on a plateau, does your church have a sense of urgency to address it? Why or why not? Jesus had one plan to reach people: the church. Jesus doesn't have another plan! Are we working God's plan? If not, what will it take to create a sense of urgency to once again work on the plan? How many new people has your church reached this year? What are their names? Have you invited them to join you for a meal?

Are we living in the dead past instead of living in a new future? Sometimes urgency (financial crisis, reduction in pastoral compensation, etc.) meets us at the door. At other times, the sense of urgency has to be created. The decline may have come on so slowly, that we did not realize we were in trouble. Assessing the situation and coming to terms with the current reality may be what we need to create a sense of urgency. At the very least, being faithful to the Great Commission of reaching new people should be enough to create a sense of urgency. We just need to be reminded, constantly! Whether it is due to symptoms or to the urgency of the gospel, we must have a sense of urgency in order to gain traction.

Look at verse three of the hymn "This is a Day of New Beginnings" (UMH 383).

℞ **Daily Health Initiative 5:** How does verse three of the hymn speak to you? How might you relate it to lab tests and results for your church? Share your insights with another person from your church.

We have taken the time for critical and crucial conversations, gone on some field trips, and assessed our sense of urgency. It is now time for a diagnosis.

Chapter Five
THE DIAGNOSIS

Jesus said to the Jews who believed in him, "You are truly my disciples if you remain faithful to my teaching. Then you will know the truth, and the truth will set you free."
— John 8:31-32, CEB

Diagnosis has Greek roots meaning "to know thoroughly" or "coming to know God."

When I was a child, I used to speak like a child, reason like a child, think like a child. But now that I have become a man, I've put an end to childish things. Now we see a reflection in a mirror; then we will see face-to-face. Now I know partially, but then I will know completely in the same way that I have been completely known. Now faith, hope, and love remain—these three things—and the greatest of these is love.
— 1 Corinthians 13:11-13, CEB

At this point in your journey, you have provided the doctor with your medical history; an examination has been conducted;

testing has been completed; and crucial conversations have occurred. It is now time for the diagnosis. The doctor has reviewed your history, examination results, and test results and will likely bring you into the office for a conversation. She will go over test results with you that have led to the diagnosis.

Just like the medical journey to a well-informed health diagnosis, this journey of discovery for your church will lead to a well-informed church diagnosis. It's time to name your ailment.

You can think about the diagnosis as the moment you look into a mirror and have a comprehensive look at current reality. It is when all the information has been gathered, and the condition has been named. Looking in the mirror reveals your outward appearance.

We would like to challenge you to look deeper. Part of your spiritual journey and maturity is holding the mirror up to reflect your faith and your soul. Remember, diagnosis means knowing thoroughly or coming to know God. Have you personally come to know God? How about the congregation? What might this deeper reflection add to the diagnosis?

Every struggling church can choose its future with dignity by actively trusting in these three assurances: God's power is made perfect in weakness, new life is possible, and death is not the end. Nothing is assured if we choose to do nothing. Buildings don't last; we are merely stewards.

A steward holds on to something at God's pleasure. What does that mean to you? For your church?

Determining the Diagnosis

Let's explore three possible diagnoses. After contemplating your answers to the questions in the first few chapters, which of these three small churches best describes your church? (1) Not Yet Big; (2) Stable, Small Church; or (3) Getting Smaller Church?

After you hear and discern the conversations, you can determine which kind of church you are in. Using the descriptors you circled in the chart in chapter one, identify where your church lines up in the chart below. Your history, gathered information, field trips, and conversations will help you identify your current church type, too. Study the chart and discuss it with other leaders in your church. Come to a conclusive understanding of your diagnosis.

Smaller Church	Was—remembering	What we did	What God called us to do	past	Looking back	Calendaring
Stable, Small Church	Is—working	What we are doing	What God calls us to do	present	Looking at today	Ministry planning
Not-Yet-Big Church	Is to come—dreaming	What we might do	What God is calling us to do	future	Looking forward	Strategic planning

When we ask this question in local churches, they often like to place themselves between two of the groups. (For example, "We are stable but tending toward smaller.") For now, choose one of the three. Now that you have made your diagnosis, let's take a closer look at each type of small church. It may help you confirm your diagnosis to gain more insight into the distinctions among the three types of small churches. Below are some descriptions you might find helpful.

Not-Yet-Big Church

If you have identified your church as a "not-yet-big church," you're likely on an upward trajectory. Maybe you have just begun a new church life cycle, and your community or mission field is growing. There is some momentum and energy in your congregation. People are excited about the future. At the same time, the church may just be stuck. Some of the resources and tools to reach more people may be missing. The spirit of possibility is present, but the church might lack the vision to make it happen. Passion may be present in some of the leaders, but matching that passion with the gifts of the congregation could be a missing link. The church may be struggling to know the needs of the community and how the church might meet those needs. In a not-yet-big church, people have the drive to do new things to reach new people. Often, a not-yet-big church is missing the compelling vision that provides focus.

Stable, Small Church

If you have identified your church as a "stable, small church," you are most likely a hard-working, loyal church doing good work. Stable, small churches are often found in rural areas or in urban/suburban areas providing an alternative to larger churches where people can get lost. Some people prefer to be a part of a smaller, more intimate church. There is a need for stable, small churches. Stable, small churches can be healthy faith communities where people grow in faith and are faithful servants in their communities. A stable, small church shares current news and information, but is not much ahead of the curve for long-term planning. In January, you plan for the upcoming year. You are most likely well-known in your community for one or two signature ministries. Your church gains a few people—mostly churched people moving into the community—as it loses a few people—mostly from transfers out and deaths.

It is possible to move from being a "stable, small church" to a "not-yet-big church." Look at your community demographics. If you are in a growing area, your church, with some changes, could move into the "not-yet-big" category. To shift into this new future, your church needs to cast a new, larger vision. It needs to determine what changes in its current structures and ministries need to take place to reach a new, growing demographic. Worship, hospitality, connection, and discipleship are some possibilities for retooling. Is your church willing to live into a new vision and make the changes needed to reach new people?

Some stable, small churches used to be much bigger churches, but experienced a period of decline at some point. The remaining members are exhausted from trying to do all the things they did when the church was larger. They want new people to help carry the load of all the ministries and programs. No one is willing to prune someone else's favorite program or pet project, so the church is doing far too many things for the number of people in attendance.

Smaller Church

If you have identified your church as a "smaller church," you are likely seeing a steady decline in attendance. The congregation reminisces about the "good ole days" and the way things used to be. If you consider the trajectory of your decline, you can probably pinpoint the day when the last person left will turn off the lights. Most smaller churches are in denial about their decline. The church is mostly reactive to the urgent needs of the day. The planning of a smaller church focuses on calendaring, often simply copying last year's calendar over to this year. **A smaller church is getting smaller each day—in both numbers and mindset**. A smaller church is focused on the care of its existing members and has lost vision and motivation for reaching new people in the community. Maybe the congregation is just tired of trying harder and getting fewer results. A smaller church typically **has no signature ministry**. It does not necessarily have a bad reputation in the community;

more likely, it has no reputation in the community. No one outside the church would notice if the church closed. The church is in survival mode with limited resources. Perhaps the building is too large for the shrinking congregation, and so there is a larger financial burden on church members. This results in deferred maintenance issues and worshiping in a space that feels large and empty. If and when people visit, they find a caring congregation, but something just doesn't feel right. Most likely, there is not a place for new people to fit in and grow in their relationship with Christ.

If your church is a "smaller church" and you desire a different future, you do have options. The possible pathways forward are outlined in the upcoming pages. But let us offer a precaution: Any decision needs to be wrapped in prayer. This is not merely a "head" decision. This is a decision of the heart and soul.

Home Remedies

Some people choose home remedies for ailments. This is true of churches, too. This might include the selling or reduction of tangible assets. (For example, a church might agree to a cell tower being placed on the property for revenue, sell the parsonage, sell off extra property, downsize staff in number, hours and salary, ignore or defer maintenance, join with other churches to share resources, assign lawn service or cleaning service to volunteers.) It's like turning off their open sign to save money.

These home remedies often patch up the problem as a temporary stop gap. The home remedy gets the church through the year. The home remedies rarely have a turn-around strategy as part of the treatment. Sometimes the home remedies are like hospice care—just keeping the patient comfortable until end of life. These smaller churches use up resources in order to survive, but they are not accomplishing the mission of the church. When smaller churches combine with other smaller churches, they are postponing the inevitable. They are not dreaming of a new future. They are simply putting a pause on death. Merging with another smaller church often undermines the mission and maybe even dilutes individuality. Mergers between two smaller churches often mix nonmultiplying culture with other nonmultiplying culture, expecting somehow to end up with a multiplying culture. (Vital mergers are a different solution—not to be confused with the typical merger where one church moves in with another. For information, see *Vital Merger: A New Church Start Approach That Joins Church Families Together* by Dirk Elliott.)

Bottom line: Typically, home remedies do not treat the the root cause. They treat the symptoms. Therefore, we do not recommend home remedies as a treatment plan for smaller churches.

℞ **Daily Health Initiative 6:** For the next week, seek out one person daily and share your small-church descriptors. Help that person understand the diagnosis. Pray about God's treatment plan for your church.

See verse two of "This is a Day of New Beginnings" (UMH 383). How do the lyrics from verse two of "This is a Day of New Beginnings" speak to you in terms of church diagnosis? Reflect on the words and share your thoughts with someone else at your church.

Now that your church has a diagnosis, it is time for treatment. In the following three chapters, you will find a treatment plan for your specific diagnosis. If you are a "not-yet-big church," go to chapter six. If you are a "small, stable church," jump to chapter seven. If you are a "smaller church," jump to chapter eight. Turn to the appropriate chapter, and let's discover your treatment plan.

Chapter Six

TREATMENT PLANS FOR NOT-YET-BIG CHURCHES

Professions of Faith Keep the Doctor Away

> The believers devoted themselves to the apostles' teaching, to the community, to their shared meals, and to their prayers. A sense of awe came over everyone. God performed many wonders and signs through the apostles. All the believers were united and shared everything. They would sell pieces of property and possessions and distribute the proceeds to everyone who needed them. Every day, they met together in the temple and ate in their homes. They shared food with gladness and simplicity. They praised God and demonstrated God's goodness to everyone. The Lord added daily to the community those who were being saved.
>
> —Acts 2:42-47, CEB

What might we learn from the Scripture above? Could the Scripture be a treatment plan for not-yet-big churches? Let's unpack it a bit.

It begins with "the believers devoted themselves." We must devote ourselves to the treatment plan. The Scripture tells us that the believers were devoted to the apostles' teaching—intentional faith development; to shared meals—radical hospitality. They gathered in the temple, praised God and prayed—passionate worship. The believers shared everything—extravagant generosity. They devoted themselves to the community and demonstrated God's goodness to everyone–risk-taking mission and service. The believers practiced what Bishop Robert Schnase described in his book, *Five Practices of Fruitful Congregations*. They were devoted to the purposes of the church. They were a living example of what we believe Jesus intended the work of the church to be.

℞ **Daily Health Initiative 7:** Each day for a month, as you prepare and share a simple meal, exchange your gladness with one another. Read and discuss Acts 2 around the table. At least once each week, invite someone to this table who is not part of any worshiping community.

Treatment Plan One: Vision and Planning

If you are a "not-yet-big church," it may be time to cast a new vision to take your church to the next level. Vision gives a clear picture of your preferred future. It provides energy, motivation, increased giving, and common focus/purpose. Vision builds consensus! Remember the life cycle of a church? It takes vision to drive church growth and start a new life cycle. Rather than concentrating on what you have been doing, visioning asks you to step back and prayerfully consider why you are doing what you are doing. If your current vision is not providing excitement, clear purpose, or momentum, it is time to reconsider the future God is calling you to.

What is God's preferred future for your church? A vision is God-given to a community of faith, often first discerned and cast by the pastor and then confirmed by the leaders. Visioning is a matter of the heart and not the head and is done best wrapped in prayer. We all know that the older we get, the more we need to stretch, but the less we do. Stretching makes us more flexible and can even make us stronger. A new vision stretches the congregation to increase its reach into the community.

As a "not-yet-big church," you are poised to move forward in faithful, effective ways to reach new people. What was your most recent Easter worship attendance? This attendance is a clear indicator of what your potential worship attendance can/should be in three years. What ways do you need to plan to allow, promote, and encourage this growth? What shifts should be made to prepare for this growth? In boating, throwing out the anchor to propel the boat forward to a desired location is referred to as *kedging*. What kedging needs to occur in your church to live out God's vision and future?

Your church will need to make sure it is doing long-term strategic planning for the next three to five years with specific plans for worship and ministry for the upcoming eight to eleven months. What are the implications for ministries, staffing, and facilities? Continue to look and kedge forward!

Below are some best practices for planning for your church:

1. The pastor and leaders meet in the fall and set church goals for the upcoming year that will allow the church to grow

into its God-given vision and remain faithful to the mission of making new disciples. (You can't have your planning meeting in a year that has already started and expect significant change!) Communicate these goals to the congregation. Keep them in front of the people who will help achieve them. Celebrate wins! Pray!

2. The board is accountable to Christ for the mission. The board/council holds the pastor accountable for the goals and vision. The pastor holds the staff and ministry leaders accountable for objectives or strategies to meet the church goals.

3. Ideally, the pastor and the worship design team hold three worship planning retreats:

    a. January Retreat: Planning preaching and worship for August–November. This is the back-to-school season through Thanksgiving. December is a time to reflect and evaluate. Then you meet the next January to plan again. This gives the rest of the staff and lay team members time to plan and be more creative.

    b. May Retreat: Planning worship for Advent–Easter. April is a time to reflect and evaluate.

    c. September Retreat: Planning worship for post-Easter–July. August is a time to reflect and evaluate.

4. To begin living as an Acts church, the pastor could start preaching from Acts, using the opening Scripture for reference and guidance. *From Members to Disciples* by Michael W. Foss (Abingdon Press, 2007) is a good resource.

Treatment Plan Two: Multiplication

Small churches often suffer from "single cell" anemia; that is, small churches are stuck in small thinking that doesn't consider multiplication. Single cells resist change and do not multiply. How do we challenge ourselves to be an organization that is multi-cell? The church might need to start a second worship service. A second service could raise worship attendance by twenty percent because people may become more regular in attendance when they have options. When people get stuck in a single-cell way of thinking, the concern of not seeing one another trumps any possible growth. If we move into multi-cell thinking, we realize we are not here to see one another, but to see God!

You cannot grow a church more than you grow the leaders to lead it. You must multiply leaders to multiply the church. You must have an intentional plan to identify, recruit, equip, and deploy leaders of today and tomorrow. What is your plan for leadership development? See *Gear Up: Nine Essential Processes for the Optimized Church* by Kay Kotan (Abingdon, 2017) to help you think through a leadership development plan and other needed processes (aka gears) to support and grow your church. Other processes and systems needed include worship planning, hospitality, connection, faith development, congregational care, new relationship building, and accountability with simplified structure.

As pastors and laity leaders, we must place ourselves in continuous learning environments.

- What are we reading to expand our thinking and learning?
- Who will challenge us to think bigger and/or differently?
- How are we studying together with clergy and laity to think and act on the cutting edge of church vitality?
- What workshops are we attending with leading church thinkers and innovators?
- Whom are we personally and corporately discipling?
- How are we raising up new believers and future leaders?

Unless we place ourselves in expectation and accountability for continuous learning, we will lose ground and become irrelevant to our culture and community.

We must put processes in place for expected growth, and we must have the staff to prepare for the growth. If we don't, we will not be able to handle the growth, and that may actually cause decline. Staff who spend their time finding new people and celebrating with people foster growth.

It is far easier to add to than take away. Young leaders often think their job is to take away, but sometimes this move backfires. Instead, once you prove you can add something, then you have the currency to take away. Addition gives you the currency to subtract. For example, a pastor starts at the church in the summer and sees that the early worship service has a small attendance. The tendency would be to want to discontinue that service and then start a different kind of service to attract more people. One pastor stopped the early service and cut giving in half. We find it is easier to add a service than to take one away. You simply cannot do it in reverse order!

There is a time when a church will reach a capacity for one-on-one relationships. Depending on which research you follow, that number could be fifty to seventy (referred to as gravitational community by Dave Pollard) or as high as 150 (per Robin Dunbar). See "How Many Relationships Can We Manage?" by Dave Pollard (http://howtosavetheworld.ca/2010/03/10/how-many -relationships-can-we-manage).

Carey Nieuwhof cites the Barna Group's statistics: "The Barna group pegs the average Protestant church size in America at 89 adults. 60% of protestant churches have less than 100 adults in attendance. Only 2% have over 1000 adults attending" (Carey Nieuwhof, "8 Reasons Most Churches Never Break the 200 Attendance Mark," careynieuwhof.com). What can we learn here?

It seems to us that there is a link between these two facts. When church attendees are connected only with the pastor, the pastor quickly maxes out his/her capacity to build more relationships. The congregation must connect with one another in a deeper way than they connected with the pastor. If the church cannot overcome this barrier, it is destined to remain a small church, never breaking the barrier of more than about 100 people. When everything, including relationships and ministry, is dependent on the pastor, the church is a "pastor-centered church." Pastor-centered churches are destined to remain small. If the church can evolve into a pastor-led congregation (pastor as leader and equipper), it is much more likely to become a bigger church. The pastor is able to spend time connecting people to one another, *netweaving*, to move beyond traditional networking with the pastor as the center of the web. Sometimes this limitation comes from the pastor's style and sometimes from the neediness and expectations of the congregation. Helping pastors to see and understand the need for different types of leadership as the church grows is essential. What got you to one size might keep you from getting to the next.

Treatment Plan Three: The People Factor

There are several key dynamics essential for growing a "not-yet-big church." Many of those dynamics are on the people side of the equation. Putting these dynamics into play is an integral part of setting the pace, tone, and expectations for growth, vitality, and faithfulness to the mission.

If a pastor is going to lead change, there must be at least three laypeople who have the pastor's back and support the change. They are advocates and mature followers of Christ who understand the mission of making disciples. Simply stated, these are the people who "get it." Bishop Sue Haupert-Johnson says she always looks to identify the seven saints of the church who will help the church move forward. We have found that whenever we are about to make significant changes, we need to turn up the heat with pastoral care so that people will not feel left behind in the midst of innovation.

Pastors and leaders must invest in key people who are committed and can help rally others to follow in a new direction. These people are likely your next generation of leaders, which has more to do with attitude than with age. Invest wisely in those you can bring along. Do not get caught miring yourself down trying to bring along people who are stuck and not willing to consider a new future. Continue to pray for these folks, but use your limited resources of time and energy to invest strategically. An excellent resource is *Necessary Endings: The Employees, Businesses, and Relationships That All of Us Have to Give Up in Order to Move Forward* by Henry Cloud (HarperCollins, 2011).

Set bars of excellence with people at all levels. When Phil Schroeder arrived at the Stark UMC in 1992, one of the older members gave him a tour around the community. He told Phil, "Preacher, before you got here, we had some highs and some lows at this church. But with you, we want to find a happy mediocre." Now Phil knew the man meant happy medium, but we cannot be satisfied with "happy mediocre." Creating an expectation for excellence brings hope. Mediocrity does not.

Offer opportunities with few or no barriers for those interested in joining the life of the church. At the same time, raise the bar of expectation for membership. Membership is about taking on responsibility for the vows and growing in faith. Membership is not about privilege. Shifting this mindset is critical in changing the church trajectory. Far too often, we have offered membership with a low threshold of expectation. Let's make church membership have meaning with responsibility and accountability.

While serving as founding pastor of Covenant UMC in Dothan, Alabama, Bishop B. Michael Watson would invite church members to come to the altar on the anniversary of the Sunday they joined the church. So everyone who joined the church on the second Sunday of January, no matter the year, was invited to celebrate this anniversary by coming to the altar to pray over their membership vows in the year ahead. The members' names were listed in the bulletin for that Sunday. They were often joined by new people wanting to make those same vows. The pastor would welcome the newest members and pray for them all to be faithful to their commitments. This was not only a special invitation that marked a special time in the congregants' discipleship journeys, but it was a call to accountability for the vows taken as members. We must be clear about expectations of regular attendees and members.

Not only must we build leaders, we also must build teams to build a church. So many times, we try to recruit people through the "all-call" or "cattle-prod" approach. This is often conducted from the pulpit or even in the newsletter. It is often received as impersonal, since it is aimed at everyone. Passing the clipboard tends to have the same effect; nobody signs up. Instead, why don't we try the "ICNU" ("I See in You") method of team building. The ICNU method starts with genuine recognition of a person's gifts. Once recognized, someone points out times when the gifts were demonstrated. Then the person is asked to think and pray about using that gift in a particular ministry. The person doing the asking then follows up in a few days to check in and see what that individual is led to do with the gift. (Note that the pastor, despite being chair of lay leadership and nominations, is not always the one doing the asking.) This is a much more personal, authentic approach to team building that is focused on aligning gifts, ministries, and personal invitation. There are few things better than when someone sees a gift in you and asks you to use it for God's purposes as a part of serving God's church.

Melissa Spoelstra, in *Total Family Makeover: 8 Practical Steps to Making Disciples at Home* (Abingdon Press, 2016), cites Dave and Jon Ferguson's 2:2:2 Principle for mentoring leaders and developing teams based on Timothy 2:2:

1. I do. You watch. We talk.
2. I do. You help. We talk.
3. You do. I help. We talk.
4. You do. I watch. We talk.
5. You do. Someone else watches.

Too often, we are so relieved to find someone to take on a job that we forget about equipping. Oftentimes, we guilt people into serving, but don't equip them to serve. People get frustrated and feel they do not know what they're doing or what is expected of them. By using both the ICNU method and the five steps in the 2:2:2 Principle, the right people are more likely to serve in the right places, fully equipped for ministry. While using these techniques may be time-consuming in the short run, the outcome will be so much more fruitful! People will find meaningful work for which they are gifted and equipped. This will also cause you to prune some ministries that have passed their expiration date, since no one feels called to lead them anymore.

If the church is to grow, the pastor may need to refocus priorities on the following:

1. Worship: The Sunday morning experience needs intentional planning, including sermon preparation and coordination with the worship team—both volunteer and paid, music folks, and audiovisual personnel. The more in advance the pastor plans, the more people can be involved in the

creative process. When more people are involved, they are more likely to be invested and invite others to be part of the worship experience.

2. Equipping: Focus on intentionally spending time with the right people, building relationships, and equipping leaders and staff. For example, take congregants on congregational care calls and equip them to take over some of the routine care.

3. Community: Spend time in the community with the unchurched. If the pastor is the role model for evangelism, the pastor must be out in the community building relationships and bringing people into the life of the congregation.

Is the pastor spending the bulk of his or her time in these three areas? If not, what must he/she do to have more time in these three areas? Are church leaders providing opportunities for the pastor to focus on these areas? What expectations or barriers might need to be removed or re-evaluated to allow this to happen to take your church to the next level?

Phil Schroeder

In starting a new church in Atlanta (actually replanting as a vital merger), we appointed a clergy couple. As their supervisor, I asked them to meet forty people outside the walls of the church each week. They felt it was a bit unreasonable, so I made it even more unreasonable and asked them to please email me those forty names at the end of each week, so that I could pray over the names too. Their coach then piled on by asking them to hold six to ten one-on-one follow-up meetings each week with some of the people they had met. The one-on-ones were not to promote the church, but to listen to the stories of the people and the community. After several months, I met with the clergy couple, and they blurted, "Why didn't you tell us about the forty people thing years ago? We have been pastors for over ten years and we could have been doing this all along. Instead, we spent most of our time inside the walls of the church, managing the people already there. Thank you for challenging us to do this. The people in our community tell us that we know so many people. We are even introducing neighbors to neighbors! How can we get other pastors to start doing this?"

Slippage Warning

As you begin to grow into a larger church, monitor these warning signs of your "not-yet-big-church" losing the battle to become a larger church. If you are not careful, your "not-yet-big-church" may start becoming a smaller church.

Top Ten Warning Signs

1. Policies and procedures begin to trump people.
2. The pastor is asked to spend more time caring for the people already there.
3. Fears rise that growth will cause us not to know everyone.
4. Burnout due to lack of new leader development.
5. Desire to return to the past because we aren't holding tight to the vision.
6. People settle into personal preferences rather than God's preferred future.
7. People care more about how things are done than about their effectiveness.
8. There is a fear of new people "taking over."

9. Members worry that new kids will cause scuffs on the walls/floors and their parents will spill coffee in the sanctuary.

10. There is a preference of honoring the dead and gone rather than living into a new future to reach the next generation.

Reflect on the second half of the third verse of "This is a Day of New Beginnings" (UMH 383).

How does the verse speak to you? What are you learning about yourself and the church in this process? Share with another person from your church.

Chapter Seven

TREATMENT PLANS FOR STABLE, SMALL CHURCHES

*Now you are still not up to it because you are still unspiritual.
When jealousy and fighting exist between you, aren't you
unspiritual and living by human standards? When someone
says, "I belong to Paul," and someone else says, "I belong to
Apollos," aren't you acting like people without the Spirit? After
all, what is Apollos? What is Paul? They are servants who
helped you to believe. Each one had a role given to them by
the Lord: I planted, Apollos watered, but God made it grow.
Because of this, neither the one who plants nor the one who
waters is anything, but the only one who is anything is God
who makes it grow. The one who plants and the one who
waters work together, but each one will receive their own
reward for their own labor. We are God's coworkers, and you
are God's field, God's building.*

—1 Corinthians 3:3-9, CEB

We are God's partners. You are God's partner in your community. We are better together. This is often signified by some youth groups in how they grasp one another's hands during prayer time and the sending out. The youth form a circle and cross their arms in front of them before grabbing their neighbor's hands—a cruciform. That formation, although simple, is one of strength, making it difficult to penetrate. When they leave, they raise their hands in the air, and the whole group turns to face outward.

A stable, small church is in itself a cruciform. Often, stable small churches share and pass the power well and in healthy ways.

℞ **Daily Health Initiative 7:** Each day for a month as you prepare and share a simple meal, exchange your gladness with one another. Read and discuss Acts 2 around the table. At least once each week, invite someone to this table who is not part of any worshiping community.

Stable, small churches have most likely become a vital part of the community. If the church were to disappear tomorrow, it would leave a huge hole in the life of the community. Since this community connection is so critical, let's explore strategies to strengthen this connection. How can you best work together as a congregation to tend to God's mission field? Stable, small churches are vital links in the community. How do you maintain that stability or, perhaps, even build on it? Because of the natural attrition due to such things as deaths and moves, reaching new people just to remain stable is critical. Let's explore some treatment plans that will allow your small church to remain stable and vital.

Treatment Plan One: Signature Ministry

What is your signature ministry? Often churches try to do too many things, being all things to all people without doing any ministry with excellence. Churches are filled with good people full of the best intentions. It is through those good intentions that we sometimes trip ourselves up. Small churches try to do too many things for too many different people. When this occurs, we are usually providing ministries that are just okay—nothing really excellent. We are often tiring our servants and burning people out. Vital, small churches do one or two things really well and are known for them in the community. You can spend a whole lot on good ideas, but you have the capacity to do only a small number of godly ideas that have servants and leaders attached to them. Mike Selleck, retired United Methodist minister from North Georgia, taught us there is a difference between a good idea and a godly idea. A good idea comes from someone's brain, and there are a lot of good ideas out there. A godly idea always comes with a leader and servants attached. If there are no leaders or workers, the idea is not yet in God's time. We need to be able to say "yes" to the right thing and "no" to the others. How can we provide one key ministry with excellence and allow other programs and ministries to fall away?

It is ironic that many of our new large churches have discovered the magic of doing one or two things really well. Many of our other churches (often, declining churches) are still trying to be everything to everyone. Think of it this way—another nugget from Mike Selleck: The United Methodist Church is still trying to sell albums when the culture is buying MP3s. We stopped asking our people to be loyal to The United Methodist Church (or to buy the whole album), but we keep operating as though people are loyal to all of our programs across the age levels. People pick and choose what they seem to need from a variety of churches. Our recreation ministry that used to be evangelism is a place for Christians to play basketball at a reduced rate. Our preschool used to be the best side door into the worship life of our church, but now it is full of children from the church down the street that only does worship and missions.

One church I recently worked with had over half the children in the preschool indicate that they did not have a church home. This stable, small church with a signature preschool is now working to connect with those almost sixty families.

Your church may not be able to give up all you are doing and do one thing, but you can choose one thing to focus on and do it really well. For example, focus on the mission of making disciples for the year and all ministries use the missional focus. Encourage your church to choose a focus for the coming year that highlights your strongest ministry. The more effort and energy it puts into this ministry, the less time it will spend trying to prop up ministries that are past their prime.

We must be willing to prune. If we don't prune, we will get some growth, but it won't be stable growth. One method to begin this process is to start with zero-based calendaring. With zero-based calendaring, we are not held captive by the same things we have done for years or decades (history and tradition). We seek to discover the one or two signature ministries that our church has the passion and gifts to offer that meet the community needs. We might start the process by asking ourselves this question: "If we were to do nothing that we have ever done before, what is the one thing we must put on the calendar?" Go deep with one ministry rather than trying to go wide with lots of ministries that do not really touch anyone or make an eternal difference. Jethro reminded Moses of this very thing:

> Moses' father-in-law said to him, "What you are doing isn't good. You will end up totally wearing yourself out, both you and these people who are with you. The work is too difficult for you. You can't do it alone" (Exodus 18:17-18, CEB).

Alice Rogers, pastor of Glenn Memorial UMC on Emory's campus, reminds small churches to use their compass. They have often lost sight of what is right around them. What is right around the church in close proximity? She asks churches to simply look to see what is to the north, south, east, and west of their congregation. Sometimes what God is calling us to is right in our backyard, but we have been looking far and wide for something else.

Folks, let us just take a moment to face the truth. Sometimes we disguise the true purpose for an activity or program in our church as something else perhaps "more churchy." The most common violator is the church fundraiser. We often kid ourselves by stating we are holding a dinner, craft sale, bazaar, or pie sale for "outreach." But are we really? Or is it truly the opportunity to ask the unchurched people we are trying to reach to fund the church budget or perhaps even the evangelism fund? Think about it. They will know we are Christian *not* by our fundraisers. Do they know we are Christian by what we sell? (In fact, many church fundraisers are only transfers from one pocket to another where I bake something for the bake sale and end up purchasing something as well.)

Treatment Plan Two: Move out of the Family System

Many times, we find small churches operating and making decisions like a family—not like organizations. If we want to break out of the stable, small-church phase and into "not-yet-big church," we have to use a new model. Organizations make decisions based on their mission and vision. The organization does not exist for the comfort and satisfaction of the family or its members. Is your church driven by compassion for a few or by a God-given vision? Does the church have a passion for being stable? It will take vision to become a not-yet-big church. If we are not careful, we could easily begin to turn the tide into a smaller church. When our own comfort is a primary driver, it will turn us into a smaller church. Live into your future with intention. We don't have to just allow the future to occur. We can live into the intention of being a stronger small church or even a not-yet-big church! We can, with the guidance of the Holy Spirit, choose!

Sometimes a stable, small church provides the opportunity or takes on the role of being a safe place and/or training ground for pastors to try and maybe even fail. The gift of stable, small churches is survival. They survive sometimes in spite of their pastoral leadership. On the other hand, sometimes small, stable churches are the product of a clergyperson at the time. Sometimes a new, energetic person uses his or her gifts to bring stability to a small church for a time.

Small, stable churches are not trying NOT to grow. They are truly doing the best they can. They are stable. Maybe your small, stable church is in a declining area. But in spite of that fact, the church is stable and a vital part of the community. There is no value judgment on the size of the church. There can be large gatherings that are chapels and clubs and small gatherings that are making disciples and changing their communities for Christ.

As a small church, we must believe that God gives us the growth. Our job is to be faithful. How would you describe the fruit that is expected to be produced as a result of your church's ministry? What kind of harvest are you reaping? Is there a bountiful harvest? Or is the harvest scarce? If your church is experiencing budget issues, you might not be producing much fruit. Money follows vision and fruitfulness. When people see you accomplishing the mission, they will fund it gladly!

Treatment Plan Three: Remain Stable and Share Your Story

Small, stable church facilities are sufficient. They are not a drag or a burden. They may not be the most modern or updated, but they are sufficient for the ministry. They do not provide a financial drain on the congregation. Stable, small churches are good building stewards and keep their buildings maintained and clean.

If yours is a small, stable church, but you want it to grow into a not-yet-big church, see chapter six. After you have mastered the treatment plans in this chapter, begin to take on the treatment plans for the not-yet-big church. These treatments will help you begin to transition into the next level of church. On the other hand, make sure you do not slip into being a smaller church. Take a look at the warning signs at the end of this chapter to help identify when a slip is starting, so that you can quickly course correct.

We sometimes have not equipped small, stable churches well (and other sizes, too). One treatment plan to shore up the stability is to help people become more comfortable sharing their faith stories. A helpful resource for pastors, leaders, and members who are struggling to talk comfortably about their faith is *Get Their Name: Grow Your Church by Building New Relationships* by Kay Kotan, Bob Farr, and Doug Anderson (Abingdon Press, 2013). This step-by-step process helps you begin to identify your faith story and then share it in safe places. It also provides steps on how people become twenty-first century missionaries to share Jesus with new people.

New people have a place at the table—but maybe we need to set out some more chairs. Stop having a kids' table. If we wait too long to bring along the next generation, they will leave—before they get to the adult table. Create a round table that dilutes hierarchy. Is there a table that creates dreams and visions?

Be careful that you are not denying the data that would lead to a misdiagnosis. You may think you are stable, but you are getting smaller. Sometimes we start slipping and don't even realize it is happening. Make sure your stable, small church does not slip into becoming a smaller church. Here are some warning signs:

Top Ten Warning Signs of the Stable, Small Church Getting Smaller

1. Worship attendance is in decline.
2. Easter attendance has declined in each of the past three years.
3. There are not enough volunteers.
4. There are not enough leaders.
5. The church is experiencing financial pressures, stress, and/or difficulties.
6. The church is beginning to defer building maintenance.
7. The preferences of existing people are considered over reaching new people.
8. There is a general lack of energy and excitement.
9. There is conflict or apathy in the congregation.
10. There has been a cut back in pastoral hours due to the compensation available.

Reflect on the second half of the third verse of "This is a Day of New Beginnings" (UMH 383).

How does the verse speak to you? What are you learning about yourself and the church in this process? Share with another person from your church.

Chapter Eight

TREATMENT PLANS FOR SMALLER CHURCHES

". . . Therefore, listen carefully. Those who have will receive more, but as for those who don't have, even what they seem to have will be taken away from them."

—Luke 8:18, CEB

Not Choosing Your Treatment Plan

How many times have you gone to the doctor and didn't like the prescriptions written or the treatments offered—even if you knew they were good for you? We often overlook the treatment, knowing full well we are destined for an undesirable outcome. It is only when crisis occurs and we are rushed to the emergency room that we are forced to choose. In the life of your church, it is far better to choose a treatment than to be forced into treatment through crisis. It's always better to choose than to be forced to choose.

Even in not choosing, we make a decision. We allow a future to reach us, even if it is not our preferred future. For example, a small church, really no more than a Sunday school class, decides to continue on being the church even though it no longer has any impact on the local community and has not introduced anyone to Jesus in more than ten years. The group is postponing the inevitable. In those same circumstances, one church might decide to move together as a Sunday school class to another church, allowing a new church to be planted inside the old location, allowing new fruit to be harvested by other harvesters.

Sometimes the building drives decisions, not the mission field. Treatment plans are held hostage by the building or the value placed on the building. We decide that the building is the church rather than the congregation. Even decisions about the building—paint colors, carpet selections, technology installation, a cross being moved—divide the congregation. We get so caught up in the facility, that we forget about the purpose of the building. The building exists as a tool to reach new people and worship God, yet we get so tied up in the aesthetics of the building, we lose sight of its purpose.

The fear of the unknown might keep a church from choosing a treatment plan. Instead of walking out in faith, the church hunkers down and sticks with its known existence, eventually dying. The fear of change is greater than the known decline that the church might already expect—even though the church will become unsustainable. Many congregants may desire the church to hold on just long enough so that their funeral service can be held there. As long as they die before the church does, it's not their problem.

Even the pastor serving the church could be blocking the treatment plan. Think about it. The best treatment plan for the church may actually be working the pastor out of a job. Not many pastors want to be known at the "church closer"! A church may be asking the pastor to lead them to a future that does not include him or her. Needless to say, it is difficult for a pastor to do this.

Phil Schroeder visited with a church that was down to nineteen people. Two of the members were there to say, "We are not going to keep driving back here every Sunday. We are the ones who come early to turn the heat on and make sure all the doors are unlocked. We now drive forty miles each way to come back here on Sundays. We love y'all and love this church, but our grandchildren go to the church in our community, and we have decided to start attending with them. What do you all want to do?" A discussion ensued. One person said, "Can't we just close when the last one of us dies?" After much prayer and discussion, the majority of the remaining seventeen decided they would move to a church nearby as a Sunday school class and give the building to the district to start something new. Then Phil asked the retired pastor who was serving the church what he thought. The pastor said, "I think we are fine. We don't need to do a thing." A year later, the church was closed. The people scattered, and the building was sold to another denomination that now has a thriving ministry.

Sometimes churches unknowingly choose an unintentional treatment plan. The outcome of an unintentional plan is usually just an extension of pain and suffering. It often results in no hope and no relief. It might be compared to a couple already separated, acting as though they are divorced before even entering the legal proceedings. We, as a church, have already separated ourselves from Christ. We have not "remained in Christ" and therefore we can't do anything. We have not been faithful in serving the church in its mission to make disciples. Doing nothing often wastes God-given resources on survival. This is not sacramental. Being faithful and being good stewards of those God-given resources is a sacrament. Denying what God can do is just defying grace, rather than trusting God's justifying and sanctifying grace.

Most churches do not know there are options. Churches believe they are either open or closed. But there is hope and choice. Hope and choice have to start with seeking current reality, making assessments, and choosing a treatment plan. However, there are **multiple** treatment plans.

Choose your treatment plan. When people plan, they take into consideration such things as advance directives, a living will, life insurance, trusts, long-term care insurance, and so on. Yet churches often do not have these kinds of plans. One might suggest that a church never plans having an end of life. That may be true. But, if that's the case, why didn't church leaders choose to start a new life cycle?

When churches choose to close before they have to, they do so because they are spiritually mature and realize they have lost the fuel to sustain fruitful ministry. Their hearts are still for the community. They close to create the opportunity for something new. They close because the decline in the church itself does not make a sustainable ministry possible.

Many churches know they are dying. They have tried everything they know how to do. Others believe they are ready to close, but not tomorrow. There may be special occasions to be celebrated in the building, such as a fiftieth church anniversary, a family wedding, or All Saints Sunday. Church leaders may delay closing until a pastor's retirement.

When a new pastor comes to a church, the first thing people want him or her to do is to get people back. People leave a church for a reason. The vast majority are NOT coming back. And if they leave once, they will leave again. Getting people back is not a strategy. Churches need strategies to reach new people. Some churches are not willing to choose the treatment plans that will create strategies to reach new, younger, and more diverse people.

℞ **Daily Health Initiative 7:** Each day for a month as you prepare and share a simple meal, exchange your gladness with one another. Read and discuss Acts 2 around the table. At least once each week, invite someone to this table who is not part of any worshiping community.

Choosing a Treatment Plan

Please read through all the plans before you make a choice. When choosing one of the treatment plans below, remember this: We bind ourselves to Christ in times of strength so that in times of weakness we have the strength of Christ to get us through.

Treatment Plan One: No Treatment

> *I am the vine; you are the branches. If you remain in me and I in you, then you will produce much fruit. Without me, you can't do anything* (John 15:5, CEB).

A church could have an intentional plan to do nothing. If a church knowingly chooses no treatment plan, it is living into its desired future. The church has decided there is little to no hope for resurrection in its lifetime. The church understands it has a limited lifespan. The church should know how long its resources will last to continue active ministry and choose a closing date. That does not mean there is not hope for resurrection in another lifetime, but simply that the church does not have the energy or resources to allow this version of the church to be a vital place of ministry to reach new people. This is not a bad thing. This choice takes current reality into account and embraces death. This treatment plan is not one of denial, but an intentional plan for no treatment with an end date in mind.

Treatment Plan One Checklist

1. Pray for God's guidance.
2. Project resources and closing date and plan accordingly.
3. Communicate the plan to the church and community.
4. Celebrate the history of the church.
5. Close when the resources run out.
6. Plan a service of leave-taking or deconsecration.

Treatment Plan Two: Die with Dignity

Because of this, since the day we heard about you, we haven't stopped praying for you and asking for you to be filled with the knowledge of God's will, with all wisdom and spiritual understanding. We're praying this so that you can live lives that are worthy of the Lord and pleasing to him in every way: by producing fruit in every good work and growing in the knowledge of God; by being strengthened through his glorious might so that you endure everything and have patience; and by giving thanks with joy to the Father. He made it so you could take part in the inheritance, in light granted to God's holy people (Colossians 1:9-12, CEB).

This treatment plan is about choosing when and how you close the doors. This is death with dignity. Just like humans choose hospice care, churches can choose a hospice-like plan. This is a conscious choice, not a default. That is the difference between plan one and plan two. Plan one sets a date based on resource availability. Plan two sets a date so as not to use all the resources on extraordinary measures in the last months and weeks of life. We can honor the past without living in it. Palliative care allows us to minimize pain. Churches have the opportunity to resize (pastoral support, building size) for the current situation. This is not an indefinite situation. There is a known future. Maybe the church just cannot bear the pain now, but has a planned ending. This treatment gives the church the time to manage the community grapevine by sending a deliberate message of intent.

The Die with Dignity treatment plan includes these three steps:

1. Pray.

   Rejoice always. Pray continually. Give thanks in every situation because this is God's will for you in Christ Jesus (1 Thessalonians 5:16-18, CEB).

2. Wait on what God is going to do.

   Youths will become tired and weary, young men will certainly stumble; but those who hope in the Lord will renew their strength; they will fly up on wings like eagles; they will run and not be tired; they will walk and not be weary (Isaiah 40:30-31, CEB).

3. Receive sanctifying grace (last rites).

   Don't cast me off in old age. Don't abandon me when my strength is used up! (Psalm 71:9, CEB)

The last rites are meant to prepare the dying person's soul for death by providing absolution for sins by penance, sacramental grace, and prayers for the relief of suffering through anointing and the final administration of the Eucharist, known as "Viaticum," which is Latin for "with you on the way."

Treatment Plan Two Checklist

1. Pray.
2. Have a time of waiting.
3. Have a time of preparing.
4. Have a time of receiving.
5. Design a legacy plan to deal with remaining resources.
6. Celebrate the history of the church.
7. Project a closing date and plan accordingly.
8. Plan a service of leave-taking or deconsecration.
9. Leave an inheritance for the next generation.

Treatment Plan Three: Become a Missional Church

Becoming a missional church is the first treatment plan offered that focuses on rebirth rather than death. Becoming a missional church is about starting a new life cycle and regaining optimal fitness. The church must leave the building in order to be a missional church. Missional means a renewed interest in reaching people in the mission field. It is about renewed love and interest for others.

"Write this to the angel of the church in Ephesus: These are the words of the one who holds the seven stars in his right hand and

walks among the seven gold lampstands: I know your works, your labor, and your endurance. I also know that you don't put up with those who are evil. You have tested those who say they are apostles but are not, and you have found them to be liars. You have shown endurance and put up with a lot for my name's sake, and you haven't gotten tired. But I have this against you: you have let go of the love you had at first. So remember the high point from which you have fallen. Change your hearts and lives and do the things you did at first. If you don't, I'm coming to you. I will move your lampstand from its place if you don't change your hearts and lives. But you have this in your favor: you hate what the Nicolaitans are doing, which I also hate. If you can hear, listen to what the Spirit is saying to the churches. I will allow those who emerge victorious to eat from the tree of life, which is in God's paradise" (Revelation 2:1-7, CEB).

When churches begin to dream about what it means to be a missional church, some think this means renting out their space or hosting a mission. Churches are not in the landlord business. We are in the relationship business. We are in the soul-saving business. We can use our facilities as an evangelism tool, but we have to do so with intention. Thinking that people who use your building during the week will suddenly find themselves in worship on Sunday is ludicrous. For building users to find themselves in worship, intentional relationship building and an invitation must occur.

We must get past the point of relying on and believing in passive evangelism. In our non-church-centric world, passive evangelism does not work. We must reclaim our roots and become circuit riders who intentionally go about sharing the good news.

But before people can hear the good news, they must have a relationship with the one delivering it. What great things are you willing to do to reach new people?

> *"I assure you that whoever believes in me will do the works that I do. They will do even greater works than these because I am going to the Father. I will do whatever you ask for in my name, so that the Father can be glorified in the Son. When you ask me for anything in my name, I will do it"* (John 14:12-14, CEB).

Even Jesus was able to trust that the next generation would do even greater things than he did. What is God trusting you with to reach the next generation? Most churches think they can be incrementally attractional when they need to radically missional (https://en.wikipedia.org/wiki/Missional_living).

Will you give yourselves away in research and development?

Adding a few new people will not counterbalance the losses from death and attrition. In the 1950s, as the people of Japan were recovering from World War II, the head of the Japanese railroad challenged his best engineers to double the speed of their trains to 120 mph. The engineers said it was impossible. The train cars would fall off the tracks at 75 mph as they went around curves in the mountain. The leader of the railroads asked, "Why do the trains have to go around curves?" In order to get to a speed that could bring transformation, they had to change the entire system rather than building incrementally on the past. (Source: http://www.meaningfulhq.com/smarter-faster-better-goals.html)

Treatment Plan Three Checklist

1. Rediscover your mission field and who is living there.
2. Renew the passion for reaching new people.
3. Sacrifice the familiar for what God is calling you to do.
4. Be willing to do good deeds AND share the good news.
5. Reinvent the systems of the church so they are outward focused, not merely attractional.

Treatment Plan Four: Be Experimental

What you might refer to as experimental in the United Methodist world would not necessarily be experimental for the rest of the world. Typically, United Methodists are not considered cutting edge. If we have learned anything in the past decade as United Methodists, we've learned that doing the same old things and expecting new results is the definition of insanity. What worked in the past no longer works. What worked last year might not work today. Our world is changing so rapidly that we (especially churches) have a difficult time keeping up. Because the world is no longer church-centric, we must continually try new ideas to reach new people using new strategies.

One experimental treatment plan might offer a network that provides an economy of scale for a group of small churches. Some of the best ideas for church restarts and plants have come from very unorthodox strategies. Align the strategies with the mission field you are trying to reach. Try something new and innovative. Make sure your eye is on reaching new, younger, diverse, unchurched people. Phil told his church that if they didn't like diversity, they would not like heaven. In response, there was laughter. Then he said, "If you don't like diversity, you're probably not going." The laughter subsided, but the point hit home.

To start a new life cycle, a church will most likely need to learn new skills, assess the mission field with a new set of eyes, and perhaps even look outside the denomination. Innovation may come from unlikely places. Involve pre-Christians in the community to help you reach the unchurched. Spend time in deep prayer and discernment for how God is calling your church to a new future. This treatment plan is an organic option. It comes from a deep yearning to do a new thing outside our comfort zones and most likely outside our knowing how to be faithful to reach new people in a new way.

WARNING!! Sometimes we try to pull together two smaller churches that will magically become one larger "smaller church." If you combine two groups using one of their existing buildings with the same shrinking model, it is unlikely the church will suddenly become vital. It could be just a prolonged death sentence.

Treatment Plan Four Checklist

1. Assemble a prayer team to pray for God's preferred future for your church and how to reach the people in your mission field.
2. Gain a new awareness of your mission field.
3. Study growing churches and new ideas about gathering and discipling people—leave no stone unturned.
4. Bring in outside help, such as a coach and/or consultant to help discern God's call.
5. Be flexible as you experiment. Be prepared to shift and adjust as you learn what works and what doesn't.
6. Stay focused on the mission and God's preferred future. Keep from going back to the past where things were comfortable and familiar.

Treatment Plan Five: Close and Restart

Write this to Sardis, to the Angel of the church. The One holding the Seven Spirits of God in one hand, a firm grip on the Seven Stars with the other, speaks: "I see right through your work. You have a reputation for vigor and zest, but you're dead, stone-dead. Up on your feet! Take a deep breath! Maybe there's life in you yet. But I wouldn't know it by looking at your busywork; nothing of God's work has been completed. Your condition is desperate. Think of the gift you once had in your hands, the Message you heard with your ears—grasp it again and turn back to God. If you pull the covers back over your head and sleep on, oblivious to God, I'll return when you least expect it, break into your life like a thief in the night. You still have a few followers of Jesus in Sardis who haven't ruined themselves wallowing in the muck of the world's ways. They'll walk with me on parade! They've proved their worth! Conquerors will march in the victory parade, their names indelible in the Book of Life. I'll lead them up and present them by name to my Father and his Angels" (Revelation 3:1-5, MSG).

Closing is a difficult treatment plan, but closing can provide the opportunity for rebirth. Closing that allows for an intentional rebirth is quite different from the previously offered treatment plans for smaller churches. This step calls for the confessing, reconciliation, healing, death, and baptism for the new start. This treatment option gives the church the opportunity to prepare for death and to prepare for new birth. It is a time of mourning, but also a time of celebration. Have you ever been struck by how often a life goes out of a family just as a new life is coming in?

Treatment plan five is about allowing something to die so that something new can begin. The church closes and goes dark for a period of six months or more; then it re-opens with a new name, a new pastor, and a new life. This treatment plan is like birthing a grandchild. The original church is not responsible for raising the new life. It is a great thing to have grandchildren and enjoy them and not be responsible for the diapers, midnight feedings, and college tuition.

In treatment plan five, the building stays, but it is usually gutted and renovated. An individual may still worship there when it re-opens, but the church will likely have a new style of worship in a newly designed space. The "new" is designed to reach the neighbor who is there now, not the neighbor who was there thirty years ago. The declining local church is optimally designed to reach the people who used to live there!

One of our churches recently closed in the city of Atlanta and has become the site for two other churches that had the courage to become a vital merger by selling both their properties and planting something new.

Treatment Plan Five Checklist

1. Create a plan for closing with closing celebrations.
2. Communicate the closing plan to members and constituents.
3. Implement the closing plan.
4. Transfer remaining members to another church.
5. The church will go dark, in most cases, for a period of six months or so.
6. Bring in a new leader to reach new, younger, more diverse people in the neighborhood.

7. Reconnect with the mission field.
8. Assemble a launch team.
9. Renovate the facility.
10. Rebrand/rename the church.
11. Create new worship and ministries to reach new people.
12. Preview services.
13. Re-open.

Treatment Plan Six: Close and Become a Second Site

Treatment plan six is to close the existing church and become a second site for an existing healthy church. This could be a church in the community or even outside the community. The first-site church needs to be growing and reaching new people. Your church wants to be a second site to a church that has growth, vitality, and reaches new people today. You are not trying to be a second site for a church that saw growth ten years ago or even three years ago. Churches can lose momentum and connection with their neighborhoods very quickly if they have not learned how to adapt when reaching new people. Seeking the right church with the proper DNA is a critical decision.

The first-site church also needs a team of people ready to commit to the launch of a second site. To think a church can close one day and new people will magically show up when the church re-opens sets us up for failure. There must be a launch plan with people ready to commit to the work. These need to be people who live in the community of the second location who will commit to the life of that site.

Just like in treatment plan five, the church will need to celebrate the ministries of the existing church before its closure. The church needs to go dark for a period of at least six months before the second site opens. This is a time for the community to see and experience the closing church gone. This is also a time to allow the launch team to network in the community, meet new people, and have prelaunch events. The building will likely need to be renovated, and new ministries will need to be created to reach the neighborhood. Expect a minimum of $100,000 to $300,000 or more for renovation in most cases. One church using this model was set to close after Easter and reopen the next fall. The church started to be part of the small-group ministry of the larger church for the fall semester the year before. Church members became so excited about the possibilities for ministry as a second site that they closed at Christmas and lay fallow until the next fall.

Treatment Plan Six Checklist

1. Seek a church planter or a judicatory leader who specializes in multisites to assist you in this process.
2. With assistance of your judicatory leader, find a growing, vital congregation to start a second site.
3. Create a plan for closing with closing celebrations.
4. Communicate the closing plan to members and constituents.
5. Ask members of the closing church to sign a covenant of behavior so they fully acknowledge that a second site of an existing church with a new vision and core values is being planted.
6. Implement the closing plan.
7. Transfer remaining members to another church. (Some will want to transfer to an existing church where they will be

more comfortable. The new church will want anyone who chooses to stay to go through new member classes so they understand the expectations of being part of a community-focused ministry.)

8. Transfer assets to the new church.
9. Begin the new launch process with the new church.

Treatment Plan Seven: Close and Release for New Birth in New Location

Treatment plan seven is similar to plans five and six with closing the church. However, after the church closes in the seventh plan, the assets are sold and repurposed for a new ministry in a nearby mission field. The church has discerned that vital ministry will be difficult in the existing location. Reasons could include a shrinking community, a shrinking population, a building that is too large to maintain, or church saturation in that area. This treatment plan is like a death and resurrection in a new body.

The congregation in the closing church can move to another church as a Sunday school class or small group. You can have other churches come in and court your people to help your congregation find a new place of worship. The pastor of the closing church helps individuals find a church where they now live. This is especially important because so many smaller churches have congregants who drive in from other areas to attend a church near where they once lived.

The new birth could be in the form of a brand new single location church, or it could be the second site of an existing healthy congregation. Look for a church planter who knows how to network and build teams or is currently serving on the staff of a growing, vital church.

Treatment Plan Seven Checklist

1. Create a plan for closing with closing celebrations.
2. Communicate the closing plan to members and constituents.
3. Implement the closing plan.
4. Release the assets of the closing church to the next generation to launch a new church for new people in a new location with a growing mission field.

Treatment Plan Eight: Takeover or Acquisition

This treatment plan calls for an existing smaller church to invite a thriving new church without a building to take over its building. This treatment plan is an adoption. It is not about fostering. Adoption is taking full responsibility and welcoming a child into your family; whereas, fostering is temporary care. In this plan, the smaller church is acquired by the new, thriving church.

Another way to think about this treatment plan is to consider Grandma's house. Grandma's house has become too big for just her. She can no longer maintain the house. A nice young couple comes in to remodel and start a new family.

There is a written and signed covenant that holds everyone accountable. Without a written covenant, the existing church will exert active and passive resistance to change. The written covenant allows laypeople to hold one another accountable to the behavior that is agreed upon in the covenant.

The new church will take over the facility and any building debt that remains after all other assets have been liquidated. The new church may need to renovate the facility. In addition to renovations, the new church will infuse its own branding and DNA into the mission field. Since they are already a congregation, the DNA has already been established. They are now just meeting in a new location.

When we did this with one church, the new church arrived to share worship on Palm Sunday. The new, young, growing church serves Communion every Sunday. Several of the members of the older church walked out before Communion as an act of protest. It reminded me that spiritual maturity is vital for new life to occur. Spiritual maturity does not walk out on Communion, but understands the sacrificial nature of the sacrament. In fact, several of the long-time members of the existing church "tendered their resignations as members" on Maundy Thursday. They never got to experience Easter.

As churches, we sometimes get too attached to the "stuff" in the building. We fear something getting torn up, scratched, or lost as we go about trying to do ministry. As a result, we end up creating lots of policies and procedures to protect our "stuff." One such dilemma is what to do about the coffee. In today's world, it is common for people to carry their drinks with them. Yet, so many churches don't want coffee or any sort of drinks in the sanctuary. They want to keep the carpet clean. Tom Davis, when he served Due West UMC in Georgia, summed up the issue quite nicely, "When Jesus comes back, he is not coming for the furniture!" Or the carpet! We simply cannot get caught up in the stuff of the building. The building is a place to connect with people so that—through us—they will find Jesus. Leaving and changing a building can be sad, but we need not be sorry.

For this treatment plan, the building must close for a minimum of six weeks for renovation and rebranding. During this six-week blackout, the congregation from the smaller church will be encouraged to attend worship at the new church that is coming to the smaller church building. Ideally, the people from the smaller church will even find a new small group to join. To join the new church, the people from the smaller church should be required to attend membership classes to see if they are willing to embrace the DNA of growth.

A variation of this model is to intentionally close the smaller church, sell the old building, and invest the assets from the old building into a new building.

Treatment Plan Eight Checklist

1. See a healthy, growing congregation in the area that needs a facility.
2. The existing congregation agrees to be rebranded with new vision and core values from the growing congregation that will move into the facility.
3. Create a plan to go dark for renovations and rebranding.
4. The congregation of the smaller church will worship with the larger church.
5. New combined congregations launch in the new site with the name and DNA of the larger church.

Treatment Plan Nine: Vital Merger Covenant

So then, if anyone is in Christ, that person is part of the new creation. The old things have gone away, and look, new things have arrived! (II Corinthians 5:17, CEB)

Treatment plan nine is a vital merger. This is a treatment plan like a marriage. Two or more vital churches come together in a union. The churches involved sell their facilities and plant a new church in a new place. If one church insists on keeping its facility in the merger, the merger does not usually work. The new facility needs to be on neutral ground. This also provides a new place for new people. New people tend to join new places. Think of it as a second marriage, where we have yours, mine, and ours coming together.

Please note this is a **VITAL** merger. Over and over, we have seen two smaller churches come together, and the new thing fails. Vital merger is a treatment plan for growing, vital churches that still have the passion, desire, energy, and resources to reach new people. This option might be for churches that are just located on the wrong sites (i.e., buried in a residential area) that want to come together to create a new place for new people in a more strategically located area. It takes a level of spiritual maturity and a pioneering spirit to sell your building and create something new!

The more churches involved in a vital merger, the better. That way, it is harder to know who is "us" and who is "them." Having more people allows the congregation to more easily create new practices and new ministries. Consider this: tradition is the living faith of dead people. Tradition is a gift. We can build on tradition. Traditionalism is the dead faith of living people who say we have to do it THIS way. How can you honor tradition without getting stuck in it? We lose the ability to reach new people for Christ when we are stuck in traditionalism. It becomes more about traditionalism than it is about the mission of reaching new people.

Treatment Plan Nine Checklist

1. Seek other healthy, growing, VITAL congregations that will agree to sell their building to do a new thing in a new place to reach new people.

2. Create a plan for closing each facility with closing celebrations.

3. Create a transition plan for the new site and facility.

4. Communicate the plan to members and constituents.

5. Ask members of the closing churches to sign a covenant of behavior so they fully acknowledge that a new church is being planted in a new place.

6. Implement the closing and transition plans.

7. Form a new leadership team representing all churches to forge a new way forward.

8. All churches in the vital merger sell their facilities and land.

9. Build or acquire a new facility on a new site.

10. Open the new facility to reach new people.

A Closing Thought

Reflect on the second half of the third verse of "This is a Day of New Beginnings" (UMH 383).

How does the verse speak to you? What are you learning about yourself and the church in this process? Share your thoughts and insights with another person from your church.

Chapter Nine
CLOSING BEST PRACTICES

Painful Process

No matter what the circumstances are, it is painful when a church has to close. It is difficult to realize the church is no longer able to reach new people in vital ways. Feelings are hurt. There is mourning. Closing a church is hard. The information in this chapter includes ideas that can help ease the pain a bit or keep conflict at bay. Our prayer is that these experiences may help your church.

The Stuff

People are often angry during a church closing, especially when people swoop in and take material things from the church, even though they may have not attended in years. In one restart project, someone from the closing congregation walked into the church during the time the new pastor was touring the building and began to tear kitchen cabinets off the wall. That woman had donated the cabinets to the church, so she was taking them back!

Because of this story and many others, the church needs to make a decision about the contents of the building and create a process to deal with the material items. Someone will need to coordinate the implementation, which may include giving things away to other churches and giving items back to people. The church will need to take inventory of its contents and liquidate things in the least painful way possible.

Best Practices for Closing

1. Advertise the closing publicly. This may feel like a celebration or a funeral, but it brings closure one way or another. People who attend the closing may not have been involved in quite some time, which can upset those who have stayed with the church through the tough times. "Oh, so you show up now for the closing? If you had been here week in and week out, we wouldn't have to do this!" We suggest a separate smaller wake or graveside service for the "home folks" who have been dealing with the closing journey all along.

2. Ensure that everyone understands the model that is finally chosen and agrees on common language and understanding. Which treatment plan is being implemented? Roles? Expectations? Benchmarks?

3. Be certain that administrative tasks are standardized by judicatory leaders so that the pastor can do pastoral care for closing churches.

4. Establish a standardized process for planting new churches with the assets of closed churches.

5. Establish a protocol for dealing with the community grapevine and perception when closing a church. Try to eliminate community confusion.

6. Note that the decommissioning service *in The United Methodist Book of Worship* is not ADA (Americans with Disabilities Act) accessible. It is designed for ambulatory folks, not those unable to move about. Revise this service for those who have disabilities and ensure that it is age-appropriate.

7. Don't drag the closing out. The grief already climaxed in the decision. The church is sometimes required to sit in grief until annual conference. The closing needs to be on the church's timeline rather than on the annual conference's timeline.

8. Help members of the congregation process their grief. People often want to be mad at someone, but there is really no one to blame.

9. Understand that many people may choose not to attend the closing worship because, in their minds, the church closed months ago.

10. Note that the church needs honesty from the district superintendent or other judicatory leaders. Sometimes pastors are expected to go in and grow a church, even when it is a church that is dying on the vine.

11. Do not make the local pastor the one to approach the closing conversation alone. The pastor needs to be in the role of pastoral care. A judicatory leader needs to approach the conversation.

12. Provide ways, if possible, to create the space for funerals. "If we close, where will we have our funerals?" is a common question. Some new churches have a legacy set up where

they can create the space for funerals for the older members. This might include popping back in the altar rails, projecting the picture of Jesus on the walls, the stained glass, or the cross. It might include creating a banner to hang at funerals with the stained glass look of the old sanctuary.

13. Create a process to help let go.

"Though much is taken, much abides; and though
We are not now that strength which in old days
Moved earth and heaven, that which we are, we are;
One equal temper of heroic hearts,
Made weak by time and fate, but strong in will
To strive, to seek, to find, and not to yield."
—Alfred Tennyson, "Ulysses" (public domain)

Epilogue
WHOLE-BODY HEALTH

Your eye is the lamp of your body. When your eye is healthy, your whole body is full of light. But when your eye is bad, your whole body is full of darkness.
—Luke 11:34-36, CEB

As you have taken this journey, you have probably discovered some areas of unhealthiness and perhaps even disease. As you reflect on the Scripture above, what have you learned about whole-body health? What areas are you choosing for treatment? What are you learning? What new insights have you gained?

When we are in emergency situations, we are afraid. The situation has come on quickly and unexpectedly. Yet in hindsight, we realize we should have noticed warning signs. Maybe there were symptoms we dismissed. Maybe we self-medicated. Maybe we tried home remedies instead of our doctor's advice. Maybe others had spoken about the change in our condition, and we dismissed them. Maybe we were in denial. Sometimes it takes something really big to get our attention. Maybe that is a trip to urgent care or the emergency room. Maybe it's the doctor telling us that if we do not change our ways, there will be long-term, serious ramifications.

What is your church's wake-up call? What have you been ignoring? What do you know now that you did not know before you read this book? What can you no longer deny? What will you do with this new knowledge?

Consider this: your church is now sitting in the ER. What will you do now in light of what you know? Will you simply bring juice and crackers to the patient? Will the patient continue to decline and move to the ICU? Will the patient still not receive treatment and be placed on hospice care? Will the patient lose his life because of a non-treatment plan? Will death occur without a legacy plan? Church leaders, it is your choice. We invite you to choose with intention rather than the choice choosing you.

This *Can* Be a Day of New Beginnings

Look at the fourth verse of "This is a Day of New Beginnings" (UMH 383) and reflect on the words. How do they speak to you in light of the journey your church has taken? What type of new meaning might these words have in light of your discovery work? Share your insights with someone else from your church.

Managing the Transition

Leaders can lead change, but most struggle with transition. No matter what kind of small church you are and what treatment plans you have chosen, change is inevitable. Many times, leaders are anxious to get to the change and begin to talk about what change they desire. But leaders often forget the important first step. They forget to lead with the "why." What are you doing to bring people along with the plan? In his book, *Managing Transitions: Making the Most of Change* (page 3), William Bridges says, "Change is situational: the move to a new site, the retirement of the founding pastor, the reorganization of roles on the team, the revisions to the pension plan (budget). Transition, on the other hand, is psychological: it is a three-part phase process (letting go, neutral zone, and new beginning) that people go through as they internalize and come to terms with the details of the new situation that the change will bring about."

Bridges goes on to explain that there is the need for a four-part plan to start a new beginning: Explain the purpose behind the outcome you seek, paint a picture of the outcome, lay out a step-by-step plan for phasing in the outcome, and give each person a part to play in both the plan and the outcome.

Final Note

If you are struggling to choose a treatment plan, please reach out. Sometimes this road is just too hard to journey alone. You may need some help navigating conversations. You might need help discovering your history, taking tests, deciding which field trips to take, making a diagnosis, or even coming up with a treatment plan. If you are struggling with any of these, please reach out for assistance. This is a difficult journey, and sometimes you need a travel guide. We can connect you with coaching and consulting services to assist your church in working through the process to create a new beginning. But the bottom line is, please don't just sit and wait; start the journey. May your journey be blessed!

APPENDIX

YOUR CHURCH HEALTH HISTORY

(Please give detailed responses. Take the time to research answers you don't know or are unsure of.)

Name of church:

_____

Age of the church—Founding date and age of each building:

_____

Recent renovations:

_____

Mission of the church:

_____

Vision of the church:

_____

Core values of the church:

_____

Membership:

_____

Average worship attendance:

_____

Number of unique individuals who worship here at least once every 90 days:

_____

Budget:

_____

Baptisms of infants/adults this year:

_____

Small groups:

_____

Hands-on mission projects:

_____

Number of new leaders this year:

_____

Number of new members this year:

_____

Confirmations _____ Transfers from UMC _____

_____

Transfers from other denominations _____ Professions of faith _____

_____

Unique missional opportunities:

_____

Needs of our community:

_____

Present ministries of our congregation:

_____

Numbers of leaders:

_____

Style of leadership:

_____

Growth potential of the community:

_____

Fiscal and facility needs:

_____

Distance from other UMCs: _____

_____

Size of neighboring UMCs: _____

How did God lead you to this church? What is your favorite memory of your life within this church? Where do you see God leading God's church in the future?

Symptoms—Check all that apply

- ❏ Fear of Conflict
- ❏ Open Conflict
- ❏ Spiritual immaturity
- ❏ People leaving
- ❏ Decline
- ❏ Lack of leadership
- ❏ Lack of volunteers
- ❏ Staff turnover

- ❑ Financial constraints
- ❑ Maintenance issues
- ❑ Lack of trust
- ❑ Lack of transparency
- ❑ Inattention to results
- ❑ Lack of commitment
- ❑ No accountability

Other:

Describe other items that may have an impact on your church's ability to fulfill its mission:

Lift up the gifts of your church. (Location might be an example):

Ministry we are known for:

Mission:
Building:
Teams:
Leaders:
Clergy:

TESTS TO MEASURE CHURCH HEALTH

Below are some tests a church may conduct to obtain some objective measures of health:

- Membership Map: This is a test that plots where your congregation currently resides. It provides information about where congregants live and indicates how well the people in the community are connected to the church. It's also a reality check of dealing with technology. Are you willing to embrace the technology needed to provide useful information that helps your church know current reality? It also indicates how far away the majority of your people live from the church. It is difficult to get a church to engage with a community to which they commute. For help, visit MissionInsite.com.

- Average worship attendance: What is your current average worship attendance? What are the trends in the church's worship attendance over the past five years? Ten years? Twenty years? Plot your findings. Is the church growing? Has the church plateaued? Is the church declining? Sometimes churches have such a gradual decline, they don't notice it until they look at their history. Sometimes a decline is so slow that a church doesn't realize it is in trouble until it is too late. In addition to average worship attendance, healthy churches often track the number of different people who worship with a church over a three-month period. A stable average worship attendance might mask the increased reach of the church in these days when even the most active people attend less and less often.

- Statistics: What are the number of deaths? How many people have transferred out of the church or have become inactive? What are the trending numbers over the past five years, ten years, and twenty years?

- Professions of faith: How many professions of faith have there been in the congregation? What are the trending numbers over the past five years, ten years, and twenty years? With and without confirmation numbers?

- Community statistics: What are the community population trends? Is the surrounding area growing? Declining? Plateauing? What is the racial makeup of the community? Has it shifted in the past five years, ten years, or twenty years? How do the community trends compare to the church's trends? Is your church demographic a reflection of the community? What is the average age of your congregation? How does that compare to the average age of the community?

- Predictor: Your Easter attendance should predict your potential for average weekly worship attendance in three years. What was your last Easter attendance? Do you like that prediction? Why or why not? What might you need to do to grow into that potential?

- Giving records: Assemble a list of giving by age level (numbers and amounts with no names). Looking at the giving numbers by age group gives you a glimpse of your overall financial sustainability. If most of your givers are over the age of seventy, the church will not have long-term financial sustainability without serious changes or significant endowments. Next, assemble a list of the top five to ten givers (again amounts without names). What percentage of the overall budget do these top givers provide? Is this a healthy percentage for church vitality and longevity? Is a family or two providing a large percentage of the church's giving? Is the church one or two moves or deaths away from a financial crisis? What is the average given per giving unit? This number speaks to the overall generosity level of the congregation. How does this level compare to the state average? National average? How does this number compare to a tithing level of the average pay in your community? See the example below of a church's giving breakdown by age group and how that giving shifts over time.

Total Contribution Dollars in 2014 by Age Group

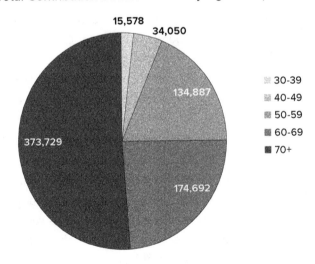

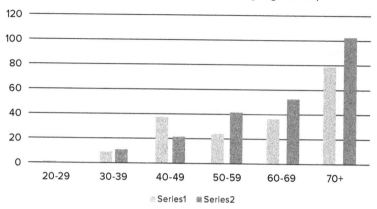

2010 and 2015 Number of Givers by Age Group

- Financials: Print or assemble a current balance sheet for your church. Make sure you include ALL church assets—real estate, checking accounts, money market accounts, endowments, trustee accounts, scholarship accounts, hold accounts, stocks, bonds, and so on. Compare the current balance sheet to the year-end balance sheets from five and ten years ago. Is there an increase or decrease in assets? Are the reserves slowly fading away? Print or assemble a current profit and loss statement. Compare that to the same statements from the past several years. What trending history did you discover? Are there fewer and fewer dollars available for the overall annual budget? Are all ministries and apportionments being funded? Is the budget growing due to an increase in attendance and thus generosity?
- Best Sundays: Take a look at the highest worship attendance Sundays outside of Easter and Christmas. When are those Sundays? What is happening on those Sundays that creates the larger attendance?

- Letter Days: What "Red Letter" Sundays do you celebrate for/with the community (i.e. teacher/police appreciation/ high school band) and "Green Letter" Sundays for the church (Mother's Day, Father's Day, and Homecoming). Bill Britt, pastor of Peachtree Road United Methodist Church in Atlanta, describes "Red Letter" days as focused on those who are not already a part of the congregation and "Green Letter" days as those focused on people who are already a part of the congregation. (Note: Most churches tend to focus only on special Sundays for themselves, Green Letter days.)

- Building usage: Who is in and out of the building on a weekly/monthly basis? Who uses the building? What are your relationships with them?
  — The church is in the relationship business, not the landlord business. How might we think about active rather than passive building activity? Passive activity is when we allow groups to use the church and think that somehow by being in the building during the week those groups might somehow decide to come to worship on Sunday. How do we expect that to happen? Will someone get up on Sunday morning and think because he or she attended a boy scout or girl scout meeting in a particular fellowship hall on Tuesday evening that he or she will suddenly have an interest in worship? At one time, this might have worked, but in today's non-church-centric world, it is naive for us to believe this will happen. If a church is to use its facility to reach new people, it must be through an active, intentional process of building *relationships* with those who are using the building. We must be willing

to offer our presence and hospitality in addition to the building.

— At Grayson United Methodist Church, the trustees met to decide whether or not to let area homeowners' associations meet at the church. They debated what to charge the HOAs to use the space. After a great deal of spirited conversation, instead of charging HOAs, the church decided to be evangelistic and offer the space for free and have someone available to greet and welcome the HOA members to the church. That same person invited the attendees to visit the church for a specific event if they did not have a church home. The diverse growth of that church can be traced back to those HOA meetings because the neighborhoods around the church were far more diverse than the church was originally. People from all over the community were visiting the church, so church leaders decided that the HOAs would meet in the church's sanctuary instead of some other space, because they wanted people to be comfortable in the sanctuary as they learned the route from the parking lot to the pew. Too often, we put visiting groups in other spaces, but getting them used to the worship space may be the first step in getting them to return to worship!

Significant Community Relationships: With what community groups does the church have *significant* relationships? (These are not places we donate to or groups we allow to use the building. These are groups we are cultivating *relationships* with on an ongoing basis.)

Churches often collect food for local food pantries. This is a good thing! Yet we often do not provide the *good news* when we do the *good deeds*. We are often passive about evangelism. Rather than donating food, clothing, blankets, and so on to some organization, could we perhaps take the next step? What if a church were to enter into a conversation with the recipients of the food and share love, concern, grace, or a prayer with them? What if churches were to build relationships with people over time so that they could share their faith stories? This is tying in *good deeds with the good news—active evangelism as we take the church to where people are rather than sitting back and waiting for them to attend.* These are not done in isolation of one another. How can we create opportunities to be on the same level as the people we are helping? How can we be the hands and feet of Christ **and** tell people about Jesus, too? How can we work with people to solve the problems of the community?

Recently, I attended a church in South Georgia where the children's sermon started with the children's minister standing at the front of the church. She had a long fishing pole with a worm dangling from her hook. The children asked what she was doing, and the children's minister said she was fishing. She said, "That is how United Methodists fish. We sit in the sanctuary and sometimes even try different kinds of bait, hoping that the fish will come to us." The children yelled, "You can't fish here. You have to go where the fish are!" She dropped the mic.

- Demographic study: Use statistics from a demographic resource such as MissionInsite.com or your local chamber of commerce to gain vital knowledge about the demographics of your community. Look at demographics such as median age, population trends, ethnicity mix, occupations, income trends, rental/owner trends, marital status, average household size, leisure time, and so on.

- Neighbors: Do we REALLY know our neighbors? Who are our neighbors? What is our neighborhood? Look at the church's neighbors, which may or may not be the neighborhood where the congregation lives.
- Many churches have become drive-in or destination churches. The people who make up the congregation no longer live in the church's neighborhood. They commute to church on Sunday, resulting in a congregation disconnected from its neighborhood. This includes a disconnect in both relationships and knowledge, with a church unaware of the general makeup of the neighborhood. We often think about our neighborhood based on how it was when we lived there rather than the reality today.
- Pioneer History: What risks did the pioneers in your church take to reach you and former generations? How might your history instruct your path forward? Who are those pioneers? What were they willing to risk? Who brought you to the church? For whom will you be a pioneer?
- Average tenure: What is the average tenure of the current congregation? Who is the newest person in the church? How long ago did that person start attending? What is the longest tenure of any one person in the congregation? What insights does this information provide?
- Method of connection: How did each person connect with the church? Born into the church? Married into the church? Already Christian? Profession of faith?

Through numerous consultations across the country, Kay Kotan has discovered that most United Methodists have either married or been born into the congregations they attend. The common method of entry into the church is transfer. The majority of those who come into the church are **not** from new professions of faith.

- Parking: How many parking spaces does your church have? Is parking adequate for the number of people attending? Expect to have 1.67 people per car. How many people can your spaces accommodate? How many designated guest spots are available? Are the guest spots the most conveniently located to the main entrance along with handicapped spaces?

One church had hit a plateau and could not understand why until the leaders counted the parking spaces. Although the sanctuary could have accommodated more people, the parking lot was full. Church leaders started parking on a grassy field down the hill from the church so more visitors could be welcomed. The church soon grew past the plateau and had to add another worship service to respond to the growth.

- Seating capacity, pew, or chair space: How many people does your worship space hold? Do not estimate or take data from an architect's word; measure actual pew lengths and divide by twenty-two inches. How many attend worship on average? Is the capacity nearing eighty percent or more? If so, it's time to start a new worship experience. Is the capacity less than fifty percent? If so, does the space feel empty during worship? Are you lacking critical mass? Lack of critical mass can lead to a lack of energy, and it can leave a guest wondering where everyone is on a given Sunday, even when the hospitality from those present is excellent.

Several churches have taken out pews or redesigned their space so it feels full more often, helping visitors to feel that the church is vibrant.

- Nursery space/capacity: What is the square footage of the nursery? What is the capacity of your nursery? Capacity is calculated by dividing overall square footage by thirty. How many children are in the nursery on average? Do you have trained and Safe Sanctuary-certified personnel to work in the nursery each week? Do you have the appropriate ratio of children to workers? Is the space properly equipped, attractively decorated, easy to find, and impeccably clean?
- Families: How many families are represented in the church? Is this reflective of the community demographics?
- Children and youth: How many children (ages 0-12) attend church each week? How many youth (ages 13-18) attend each week? How many participate in leading worship on a monthly basis? Are there Safe Sanctuary-certified teachers (besides their parents) ready to teach/lead each week? Is the school district growing? Declining? Stable? Do your children's and youth ministries reflect this?
- How many first-time guests does your church have per month on average? How many returning guests? Look at the historical data and compare these numbers over the past five years, ten years, and twenty years. What trends have you discovered? What is the follow-up process for first-time guests? Returning guests?
- What major conflicts has the church had in the past twenty years? Has the conflict been resolved? Are there still grudges or concerns about the conflict?
- Faith development: Describe the process of how a new believer becomes a faithful follower of Jesus Christ. How

do members consistently deepen their faith through the life of the church?

- Pastors: How many pastors has the church had over the past twenty years? What is the average tenure? Is there anything to discover about this? If so, what?
- Age: What is the average age of the congregation? What percentage of the congregation is over age sixty? What does this reveal about the future of the church? How does the average age of the community compare to the average age of the church?

MARCIA MCFEE'S ANNUAL CONFERENCE CHURCH CLOSING LITURGY

A Ritual of Thanksgiving

Bishop: To everything there is a season, and a time for every purpose under heaven. We release what is past in trust and open ourselves to the new creation God brings.

[Repeat the following for each church:]

[*Church name*] _____ has provided refuge and comfort for God's people, servanthood and witness for its neighbors and the world.

Our hearts are filled with thanksgiving for this ministry.

[when each church has been named . . .]

Blessed be the name of God, whose Word has long been proclaimed within each of these hallowed places.
We give you thanks, O God.
Generations have prayed their prayers and sung their praises
as members and friends in these churches;
your Spirit has blessed countless worshipers.
We give you thanks, O God.
Grace upon grace nurtured people in the Lord's Supper, study, fasting and holy conversation.

We give you thanks, O God.
Bless, O God, those who are going out from each of these churches
with a continued journey of faith.
They are yours, we are yours.
Thank you for the glory of the power that is love,
forever and ever. Amen.

*(Note: This is used with the permission and encouragement of Marcia
McFee.)*

RESOURCES

William Bridges. *Managing Transitions: Making the Most of Change* (Da Capo Lifelong Books, 2009).

George Bullard. *The Congregational Life Cycle Assessment* (The Columbia Partnership, 2013).

Kennon L. Callahan. *Twelve Keys to an Effective Church: Strong, Healthy Congregations Living in the Grace of God* (Jossey-Bass, 2010).

Henry Cloud. *Necessary Endings: The Employees, Businesses, and Relationships That All of Us Have to Give Up in Order to Move Forward* (HarperCollins, 2011).

Discontinuation of Local Church Checklist, http://s3.amazonaws .com/Website_GCFA/services/legal/Discontinuation_of _Abandonment_of_Local_Church_Property_Checklist.pdf.

Dirk Elliott. *Vital Merger: A New Church Start Approach That Joins Church Families Together* (Fun & Done Press, 2013).

Michael W. Foss. *From Members to Disciples.* (Abingdon Press, 2007).

Charita Goshay, "Faith & values: New survey suggests marked decline in Christian affiliation," CantonRep.com (http://www .cantonrep.com/article/20150530/LIFESTYLE/150529155), May 30, 2015.

Kay Kotan, Bob Farr, and Doug Anderson. *Get Their Name: Grow Your Church by Building New Relationships* (Abingdon Press, 2013).

Carey Nieuwhof. "8 Reasons Most Churches Never Break the 200 Attendance Mark," January 19, 2010,

https://careynieuwhof.com/8-reasons-most-churches-never
-break-the-200-attendance-mark.

Dave Pollard. "How Many Relationships Can We Manage? *How to Save the World* website, March 10, 2010 (http://howtosavetheworld
.ca/2010/03/10/how-many-relationships-can-we-manage).

Robert Schnase. *Five Practices of Fruitful Congregations* (Abingdon Press, 2007).

Daniel P. Smith and Mary K. Sellon. *Pathway to Renewal* (Rowman & Littlefield, 2008).

Melissa Spoelstra. *Total Family Makeover: 8 Practical Steps to Making Disciples at Home* (Abingdon Press, 2016).

Douglas Walrath. *Making It Work: Effective Administration in the Small Church* (Judson Press, 1994).